ReWrite The Rules!

Turn Your Life Around
From Victim to Victorious

David Gillman

Publisher: Keystone Coaching
Sunbury, Victoria, Australia

http://www.keystonecoaching.net

Copyright © David Gillman 2019

All rights reserved. No part of this book may be reproduced or transmitted by any person or entity (including internet search engines or retailers such as Google, Amazon or similar organisations), in any form or by any means, electronic or mechanical, including photocopying (except under the statutory exceptions provisions of the Australian Copyright Act 1968), recording, scanning or by any information storage and retrieval system, without prior permission in writing from the publisher.

 A catalogue record for this book is available from the National Library of Australia

ISBN 978-0-6485432-0-6

Front cover design: Rob Williams, ILoveMyCover

Front cover photograph: Barry Ellem

Illustration in Chapter 1: Rabia Batool

Book layout: Derek Rawson

Print and Distribution: Lightning Source/Ingram

Dedicated to the children, teenagers,
young adults and their parents
who are going through dark times and seeking help.

&

With gratitude to my family, friends, foes and associates who have all
contributed to my knowledge and given me the
energy and inspiration to help others.

David Gillman is a qualified Master Life Coach. The ideas presented in this book are based on his life experiences. The reader is invited to apply the ideas while bearing full responsibility for their application and any results, and is counselled to seek professional advice in the case of serious life issues.

Note: In places gender-specific terms (such as 'he') have been used in order to make the text easier to read. Whenever a gender-specific term is used, it should be understood as referring to both genders, unless explicitly stated. No offence or sexism is intended. In other places 'they' has been used, reflecting contemporary conversational speech rather than correct grammar!

Note: Best efforts have been made to find and acknowledge the true source of all quotes. If we have got this wrong, please let us know!

ABOUT THE AUTHOR

David Gillman is a Neuro Linguistic Programming (NLP) Master Life Coach. He runs his own coaching practice, Keystone to Success Life Coaching. He has revolutionised printing practices in the presentation awards ribbon-printing industry while working in his family business, and is a three-time Australian Dancesport Champion with numerous national and state titles to his name.

The family printing business was not only a source of income and opportunity for David, but also triggered a life-changing crisis when he was 12 years old, resulting in him almost taking his own life. He achieved the extraordinary, managing to coach himself out of that one-way journey, and reapplied himself to the art of creating a fulfilling life.

In the process of healing David discovered a wondrous wealth of people and wisdom in the teachings of Neuro Linguistic Programming, which enabled him to hone his self-taught life-coaching skills. It has been David's lifelong goal to bring a message of hope to those who don't want to live in fear or despair any longer, and instead wish to live lives of significance. This book is the realisation of that goal.

"It's never too late to change the direction that your life is going in."

– DR. WAYNE DYER

"Life is not about finding yourself. Life is about creating yourself."

– GEORGE BERNARD SHAW

CONTENTS

Preface 1
Introduction 4
Chapter 1: The Four Prisons I Created 8
Chapter 2: The Brilliant Little Voice That Saved My Life 14
            Emergency and Support Information 20
Chapter 3: The Destructive Rules I Was Living By 25
Chapter 4: My New Rules, And How I Arrived At Them. 28
Chapter 5: Another New Rule: Listen To The Most Empowering Voice . 34
Chapter 6: Old Rule: Survive! 42
Chapter 7: My Pact With The Devil, And How We Both Won 51
Chapter 8: The Likely Outcome Of Living By The Rule of Violence . . . 62
Chapter 9: New Rule: Hold Onto Your Dreams
           And Let Go Of Your Illusions 74
Chapter 10: An Old 'Feel Better By Eating' Rule Is Transformed 81
Chapter 11: Old Rule: Stay In Your Comfort Zone. New Rule:
           Take A Risk! Get Out There And Invest In Yourself 96
Chapter 12: Important Friendships Are Worth Waiting For 106
Chapter 13: Strategies For Success. 112
Chapter 14: The Rule Of Creative Competition And Reinventing Oneself . 132
Chapter 15: ReWriting The Rules Of The Jungle 138
Chapter 16: New Rule: Appreciate Hurtful Experiences 147
Chapter 17: Apologies And The Forgiveness Process 157
Chapter 18: Support Systems 166
            Conclusion 173
            My New Empowering Rules 177
            I'd love to coach you! 180

PREFACE

Between 1990 and 2016 the total number of deaths from suicide was 22,433,833. In 2016 alone, the total number of people lost was 817,147. That figure encompasses all people aged five to 70+.

This shocking data comes from the Institute of Health Metrics and Evaluation (IHME). A graph tracking four age brackets reveals that the largest group was aged between 15 and 49 years, and accounts for approximately 60% of all deaths. In general, in most high-income countries, the figures also indicate that the ratio of male suicide to female suicide is three times higher.

Suicide Deaths: 2016: Total Worldwide = 817,147[1]

AGE: 5-14	AGE: 15-49	AGE: 50-69	AGE: 70+
7,975	486,294	212,294	110,643

But there is another disturbing number to consider. According to the World Health Organization's best estimates, for every successful suicide, twenty more people are attempting it. The figures published by the Centers for Disease Control and Prevention in the U.S. indicate that there are roughly 25 attempts for each suicide death. For young adults aged 15-24 the ratio is much higher: there are approximately 100-200 suicide attempts for each suicide death.

If you consider these facts, you soon realise a new possibility: unbeknownst to you, a family member, a loved one, a colleague or a friend may be considering suicide and be so affected by the stigma of shame that he or she is unable to reach out for help.

It is with this in mind that I wrote *ReWrite The Rules*. By the age of 12 I had fallen into such a state of depression that I knew I was spiralling out

---

[1] From Global Burden of Disease Study 2016 (GBD 2016) Results. Data published by Global Burden of Disease Collaborative Network, Seattle, United States: Institute for Health Metrics and Evaluation (IHME), 2017. Website: https://ourworldindata.org/suicide

of control. I had been the miserable target of schoolyard bullying for several years. I was unable to get close to the girl I had a crush on. I was grieving family pets that had recently died. And I was struggling as an only child while my parents focused on keeping their small business afloat. I just wanted a miracle to occur and return life to how it had been a few years earlier before everything 'went wrong'. I felt that if I could find a book by someone who had experienced what I was experiencing, they would surely have some advice that would help me. But my parents' library contained no such book; neither did the school library or the city library.

There are many empowering resources available on this topic now. It is my intention to add to them and do what I can to reduce those staggering statistics. This is the book I was looking for when I was 12. It is for teenagers and young adults who feel burdened by crises. It's also for their parents and grandparents and guardians. I hope you will donate a copy to your library to help me aid, empower and even rescue those in danger of taking their lives.

The personal stories I share in *ReWrite The Rules* reveal both my darkest days and the steps I took to empower myself and make the following years much more enjoyable and enriching. I've shared so honestly that I've winced, at times, at the memories of how I tried to deal with my hardest times. But I've shared those very personal stories to save you some pain.

This book doesn't just cover the topic of suicide prevention; it also addresses the issue of schoolyard bullying and revenge, the challenge of a broken heart, and other 'life journey difficulties' that ensue when you don't feel confident or worthy. It challenges you to ask and answer some probing questions with the outcome of turning your life around, regardless of what you feel up against right now. As you read, you'll come across strategies and tips for dealing with bullies and your own disempowered self-talk.

Whether you are seeking help for yourself or for someone you care about, or whether you simply want to understand the dynamics that drive someone to suicide, this book will offer value. The pain for a family of sitting down to dinner and forever facing the empty chair of a loved child is inestimable. What might that child have contributed to both the family and the world? Such pain cannot be ignored.

Imagine, also, being able to prevent a vengeful child from maiming or killing another child. The spite I felt for one of my bullies almost resulted in jail time (and all the other serious costs and consequences that such an act would have unleashed). You'll discover how I managed to pull back from a potentially disastrous act.

If we want a different result in our lives we have to behave in different ways. We can't hope for a better result if we keep doing the same old things. The first 'different thing' might be reading this book and generating a new set of ideas, strategies and personal rules.

You will receive immeasurably more from this book if you take the time to respond to the exercises offered throughout. I recommend that you treat yourself to a new, good-sized notebook and dedicate it to your journey. Be as honest as you can, remembering that the information you record is purely for your reference as you go about building a new set of rules for your life.

INTRODUCTION

"I regret nothing in my life even if my past was full of hurt.
I still look back and smile, because it made me who I am today."

– UNKNOWN

How much do you know about this guy in the photograph? Do you assume that he is lucky, successful, wealthy? After all, he's wearing tails, he's beaming, he looks like he's being applauded. Maybe he was born with a silver spoon in his mouth? Maybe he was always destined for success? Or is he just a poser? Is he just playing a role in this photo?

Could you possibly know, from this photo, that for most of his life he was tormented by one thing or another? Would you know that he almost took his own life, at age 12?

The thing about humanity is this: each person we encounter is just another face. Until we begin to interact with them, we have no idea who they are or what they are about; we have no idea if they have been cruising through life or grappling with the worst challenges.

In my case, my near-suicide at age 12 became the lynchpin to my success. My life changed when I realised that 'the universe' made everything happen *for* me, not just to teach me a lesson or trip me up.

That is a very big idea and one that might be unsettling to you. But hang in there and let me unfold it for you through the pages of this book. The key thing, however, is that whether you agree with the philosophy or not, it's much more empowering to view the challenges in our lives as being there to serve us than as 'punishments' for being inadequate.

Contemporary video games encourage children to develop the skill of thinking outside the box from a young age. Their role-play character is usually defeated in an opening round of the game, so they hit the reset button. They try again and again and again, and in the process learn to anticipate what is going to happen and prepare for it. Eventually, they understand the rules and principles of the game so well that they can pass the level easily. Then they have the option of experimenting with other strategies to develop more variety of approach.

As a 12-year-old I didn't realise that I was playing by some pretty destructive rules – and they were rules that *I* had invented or accepted! (I will explain this in Chapter 1.) At the age of 43 I now finally know why I had to survive what I did. It has taken a VERY LONG TIME for me to understand and forgive certain parties for their actions because for that very long time I was angry and focused on justice and retribution. In the end my breakthrough came when I had the following realisation:

If you allow this situation to continue to interfere with your thinking and emotions in day-to-day life, how much of YOUR life will it rob you of?

That realisation gave rise to this question:

What actions are you going to take to stop this destructive thinking, turn your life around, and free yourself of this burden?

My journey from that point was not all plain sailing. I continued to struggle and fall backwards, but my direction had changed significantly: I was headed in the direction of greater responsibility and a life that would fulfil me and make me proud.

Now I have an important question for you. Keep your answer at the back of your mind while reading the rest of the book. The question is this:

Are you free or imprisoned by rules and beliefs that don't serve you?

If you are imprisoned, have you allowed others to put you in prison or have you done it to yourself? And, most importantly, whether you allowed them to imprison you or you did it to yourself, how do you rewrite the rules of your life and set yourself free from this prison?

I have described the strategies that worked for me in simple, straightforward steps so you can apply them as quickly and easily as possible. Will my experiences and insights help you? I believe so, because success in life is not a mysterious business and it's not purely the result of chance or good fortune; success is the result of taking action on useful ideas.

During the early stages of my competition dancing career, Kerrie Ward, one of the greatest coaches I ever had, told me: "David, I have a lot of experience but I can't install that knowledge in your body. I can only impart information; you have to be the one who practises and applies what I tell you."

Travel back in time with me now. Use my life experiences to unravel your story and understand what is holding you back. And then take those insights and turn your own life around.

David and Kerrie Ward, at the Australian Dance Sport Championships, 2016

"You are always one decision away from a totally different life."

– UNKNOWN

Chapter 1: The Four Prisons I Created

> "Suppressed pain ... always comes to the surface. It shakes you into reflection and healing."
>
> – BRYANT MCGILL, SIMPLE REMINDERS: INSPIRATION FOR LIVING YOUR BEST LIFE

The last straw came when I rang Mum for help with some Year 7 French homework. She was at the factory with Dad trying to keep the doors open, and she was busy and stressed. When I asked for help she got mad with me for not trying to figure out the French by myself, and she hung up on me.

I was alone in the house. The day seemed warm for winter. I could hear children playing outside in the park. Little sparrows were chirping in the leafless branches of trees, and I was sitting in my pale white bedroom with the grey carpet staring at a possible detention for not doing my homework.

For months I had looked in the library at school, in the local public library, in my bedroom and on my parents' shelves for a book that might address issues like school bullying, broken heart, lack of energy, lack of connection with my fellow students or teachers, lack of motivation at school, anxiety, depression and suicidal thoughts. I just wanted to find a book that addressed all my problems directly and simply. I didn't want to have to wade through long stories and explanations before getting to the point. But I had found nothing.

I walked to my bedroom mirror and looked at my reflection. I was convinced that I'd been adopted because my parents seemed able to march on in their pain but I couldn't succeed in mine. I was dumb! In a massive fit of frustration, I went berserk in my bedroom. I threw my books against the walls, tore the linen off my dishevelled bed, kicked my bedroom door, threw pencils and pens everywhere, and then collapsed in the middle of my room, numb and empty.

I felt broken beyond help. The pain I'd been living with for years was getting worse. I yearned for the way things had been in my early primary school years, before everything went off the rails. I closed my eyes and wished I could move myself out of now into then, but when I opened my eyes, the pain was still there.

And then it dawned on me that I knew what to do. I calmly rose to my feet. I walked to my desk. I began to write a three-page letter to my parents explaining what was going on. I described my headmaster and the kids and teachers at school who'd been giving me a hard time. I folded the letter, left it on my desk and proceeded to the rumpus room.

In the corner there was a gun safe. I had no keys but I knew how to get a gun out of the safe using 'other means'. Gun in hand, I proceeded to a wall rack where I knew there was a cartridge. I calmly put the cartridge in the chamber then walked to the couch on the other side of the room. I sat down and thought for a moment how best to aim the barrel at my skull. I figured there were two ways.

Option Number One: Aim the barrel at the side of my skull and reach the trigger with my finger. Possible.

Option Number Two: Place the butt of the gun on the floor and use my toe on the trigger whilst aiming the barrel into my mouth. Feasible.

For some reason my next thought was of being a toddler running around at Christmas time, excited, surrounded by cousins, aunts and uncles and grandparents, my proud mum and dad watching over me. A unified friendly family. A time when my future had looked fun, happy and prosperous. A complete contrast to the cold hard end of a twelve-gauge barrel. The barrel represented finality, a dream unlived. The Richard Scarry stories I'd read as a child that had made me wonder if I would become a bank manager, policeman, taxi driver or teacher were a long way away. I was now sitting in the rumpus room considering ending my life, and I was only 12 years old...

How had it come to this? My childhood, as far as I can remember, was very happy. While I was an only child, we had regular enjoyable contact with grandparents, aunts, uncles and cousins. We lived in an eight-square house in Glenroy and had chooks and two dogs as pets. Between 1978 and 1983 I can honestly report that I looked forward to waking up each day. Mum would often say that she would walk into my room and I'd be smiling back at her, whether I was a baby, toddler or child.

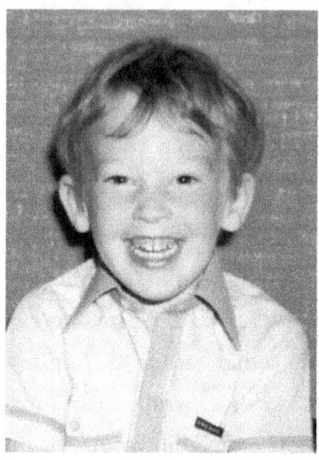

1980, David at kindergarten

My parents were running a steadily growing business in the shed out the back of the house. They were printing foil-embossed lettering on sashes and my father was innovating new machines. To my child eyes, they seemed tired at the end of every day but content. Life seemed to be fine and improving – although I was raised to some extent by the colour TV set as my parents were too busy to look after me every day.

It didn't occur to me or my family that our prosperity was being observed by a 'wolf in sheep's clothing' who, very soon, was going to sneak into our barn and wreak havoc with my family and childhood.

This character executed his plan perfectly. On a lovely sunny day in spring 1982, my mother hurried out of the new factory my parents had recently purchased for the family business to pick me up from school. As she was leaving, a man introduced himself as a factory inspector and asked to be let in. Mum had no time to pay much attention so she just pointed him through the door. My father was in there so she had no need to worry.

During his visit, the 'factory inspector' appeared to be looking at the ceiling and walls but was really looking at Dad's modified printing machines. After about twenty minutes, this 'factory inspector' left.

A year later, a new printing company started up in a nearby industrial suburb. News came to my father that the 'factory inspector' had copied the majority of the designs of his machines and was actively stripping clientele from his books.

This news changed my Dad. A once happy man, my father slumped into a depression and subsequently had a minor nervous breakdown. My mother, unable to cope with this development, also struggled. The flow-on effect struck me the following year when I began to struggle at school. I didn't know it at the time, but the depression that had beset my parents was also taking hold of me.

As the years went on, I found myself progressively 'imprisoned'.

1. The first was the Prison of Depression.

I lost my young child's confidence and optimism. My parents' depression and my years of constantly watching television affected my ability to learn and interact naturally and easily with other kids in my year at school. I began to struggle with basic subjects, and the other students began to take an interest in bullying me. When I fought back they would gang up on me either psychologically or physically, but the teachers seemed apathetic and disinterested when I reported these incidents.

During the first school assemblies I attended I was given the impression that if you obeyed the school rules and treated your fellow students well you would be rewarded, but if you treated a fellow student badly, you would be punished. These were the first rules handed to me outside my family, and I did my best to obey them. But in practice that didn't seem to be the case: in practice, it seemed that no matter how well I behaved, I always came off worse.

I appealed to my teachers for help dealing with the schoolyard bullies but was never satisfied with the outcome of their intervention. I remember walking away thinking, *'What's the use? There is no real justice.'* I hungered for justice but as far as my life was concerned, I seemed to be the meat on the table.

As a result of my depression, my trouble studying and making friends, institutional indifference and student cruelty, I found myself in…

2. The Prison of Anxiety.

The unspoken rules of the school system meant that I was constantly on the alert, vigilant and worried. I couldn't relax. Locked in this prison, my interest in the future began to wane.

As the 80s rolled on other little incidents compounded my troubles. Being excluded from house sports teams may seem like a small thing, but it was crushing to my young self-esteem. I developed unhealthy eating habits, and as my fitness and energy levels plummeted, I gained weight. Another flow-on effect was a steady drop in my school marks. This downward spiral would occasionally trigger my parents to storm into my room and demand that I pick my game up. They did not understand the extent of my anxiety and depression because I was too embarrassed to talk about it with them, and too stuck in apathy to do anything about the persistent disappointments. I began to languish in…

3. The Prison called 'Mourning'.

Between 1984 and 1988 the situation worsened. It seemed that my pleasant childhood was all but lost: a girl I'd had a crush on since kindergarten had seemingly run into the arms of one of the bullies – the one who caused me the most trouble; the dogs I'd grown up with during my childhood had to be put down within eight months of each other; my marks continued to plummet; my interest in people all but vanished; and almost all the friends I'd started out with at kindergarten had drifted away. My perpetual state of mourning from all this loss shut me in…

4. A Cell called 'Isolation'.

The isolation would be similar to being abandoned on a desert island with no hope of rescue. The body and mind weaken. Every day becomes a struggle to get out of bed, and once up, you only have energy for the most basic survival tasks. I'd walk around with my head hunched over my frame, unable to see my way out of my various dilemmas.

Depression, Anxiety, Mourning, Isolation… these emotional states had me as stuck and hopeless as if I were really in prison. At the age of 12 I would walk around school every day in 'prison stripes' that no-one seemed to either see or care about.

Then one winter day I had had enough. I still remember the date: 25th August 1988. The four prisons I'd been living in had become so toxic that I felt as if I were being irradiated by plutonium. That was the day I broke into Dad's gun safe, took out a gun, and held it to my head. Fortunately for me, the little voice of my intuition kicked in and rescued me; if it had not, I might have found myself in a 'forever prison' – a coffin underground.

Those four emotional prisons had seemingly impenetrable walls but they were self-imposed prisons. You may also discover, as I did, that you have inadvertently admitted yourself to such a prison. I say 'admitted yourself' because we are not forced to adopt certain attitudes; while our choices might not be fully conscious or desirable, they were not imposed upon us – *we decide how to think and what to believe*. It is our choice as to whether we stay in, or escape from, that prison.

In the next chapter, I will describe how I rescued myself from suicide.

"Life has many different chapters; one bad chapter doesn't mean it's the end of the book."

– ANONYMOUS

"Don't start your day with broken pieces of the past. Yesterday ended last night. Today is a brand new day, and it's yours."

– ZIG ZIGLAR

"Always remember that your present situation is not your final destination. The best is yet to come."

– ZIG ZIGLAR

CHAPTER 2: The Brilliant Little Voice That Saved My Life

"If you're searching for that one person who will change your life, take a look in the mirror."

– UNKNOWN

As I sat there with the gun in my hand, heavy with despair and dread, a little voice seemed to put a hand on my shoulder.

Look! If you screw this up, you could be a vegetable for the rest of your life and stuck in another prison!

Me: "Yeah, I know." The thought had occurred to me as I sat there with the gun poised: What if I flinch?

The little voice broke into my reflection. *Don't you care?*

"No. The pain's only getting worse. I've got to do something!"

And what do you think your parents will find when they come home?

"I don't care... I'm in too much pain!"

You don't care that when they come home, tired after trying to keep their business running and keep you in school, fed and sheltered, that they'll find your remains on the floor and your brains on the wall?

"I do feel sorry for them. But part of this is their fault! They haven't been there for me when I needed them. And they ganged up on me too! They didn't like the fact that my marks are dropping and they bullied me to study when I had no energy."

Are you going to feel sorry for yourself if this fails and you're stuck in a hospital ward the rest of your life?

"I am frightened of what might happen if this fails…"

And what do you think the outcome will be if you succeed?

"That I'll leave everybody with a guilty conscience about what happened to me!"

The Brilliant Little Voice That Saved My Life

Really? You think your parents will show the letter you left on your desk to the students and teachers who you feel led you to this?

"Yep!"

At this point, the gun was feeling too heavy for me to keep holding it poised against my head. I put it down for a moment, intending to lift it up again once my arms stopped aching. The next time it went up I would instantly pull the trigger.

Okay, so the letter is displayed or read out at school, the voice persisted, *assuming the headmaster who seems totally apathetic to you will do that in the next assembly. What then?*

"They will pay in guilt for the rest of their lives! They all know who they are."

Sure they do. And then what? What do you think will happen after they find out you've killed yourself?

"They will go on living their lives in prisons of their own! The result of what they created for me."

Really? You think their lives will come to a halt over this day?

I paused. It only took a few moments to realise that I was kidding myself. The kids at my school didn't really care about anyone but themselves and their mates. They would experience a momentary flash of shock or even guilt but then their lives would just carry on.

"Probably not," I admitted.

Do you think they'll still be caring about you when they go to parties, get married, have families and build their careers?

"Yep! They might go on but they'll always feel bad." I was trying to stick to my plan but my bravado was faltering…

No! They won't. If they haven't cared about you in the lead-up to this day, why will they care into the future?

"I guess… maybe." I paused for a few moments thinking of some of those jerks in the playground playing football, pushing other students around, having fun and dreaming about their grand futures and the adventures they wanted to have.

What use will you be then, if you don't go on past this day? How will they really learn their lesson if you're not alive to teach them?

"Teach them? No-one believes me when I cry foul! As soon as they argue back the headmaster or teachers listen to them too and no-one seems to care about what they did to me! There's no justice. No hope. No happiness. They never learn anything. Why is everyone else allowed to have happiness and success but not me?"

The little voice was not distracted by my despair. *What if we could find another way to deal with these problems?* it asked. *Maybe we could think of a way, over time, to find their weak points.*

"Maybe. But what about me? Where's my life going to go from here?"

Anywhere, as long as you're living and breathing. You can't do anything when you're dead. I guarantee you'll be forgotten by almost everybody if you die.

I paused again. I thought. I pondered. I wondered... It was difficult to see through the fog of depression but the little voice had a point. I wasn't going to be in school forever. If I could just hang in there...

"But I want vengeance for all the years they've been hurting me!"

You want vengeance? Do you want me to tell you how to get it?

"Sure!"

Take the cartridge out of the chamber and put the gun away first.

I looked at the gun for what felt like minutes. With a sigh, I broke the gun open, emptied the cartridge, sighed again, stood up and returned it to the gun case.

And now listen to this: your best vengeance is to live – and flourish! – in spite of them. Your best retribution for their wrongs to you is to take their cruelty and use it to empower yourself. The way for you to win is to come from behind and surpass them, to get up out of the dirt and succeed.

That sounded quite ridiculous and impossible to me. As I was by this stage feeling completely drained, I left the rumpus room and made myself a cup of tea. Then I returned to my bedroom and began to clean it up. I needed something simple and practical to do.

The little voice spoke again while I tidied my room: *You will never forget this day. You may not be able to forgive those people for their unkind behaviour but your decision to take the power over your life back into your own hands will push you into creating a new significant life.*

"Yeah, maybe," I grumbled. "But I don't feel significant. I'm being drowned out in this crap of so-called humanity. Why can't people be nice to me?"

The changes you are looking for outside of you need to come from inside of you. Here's what I want you to do...

Ironically my parents arrived home at that point. I heard them moving around the house but didn't go to see them. And they had no idea that a silent menace had almost stolen their son away.

The rest of this book is where I share what I learnt and how I began to slowly transform my life, but it took nearly three decades to fully realise that on that day, as a 12-year-old, I had coached myself through one of the worst crises a human being can ever face. For the first time I had realised that life was what *I* made of it, and I had the power to turn even awful circumstances around.

It turns out that the Wise Little Voice that coached me was a facet of my mind, related but not closely, to the other voice that had disguised itself as my friend but was, in fact, Depression. Depression has only one strategy for dealing with the challenges you face in life. Depression talks to you when you're tired and feel you no longer want to deal with the problems that just keep stacking up. It whispers one instruction: Retreat.

There is, of course, nothing wrong with making a strategic retreat on occasion during the course of one's life. But Depression whispers 'Retreat' in your mind almost constantly. It does what it thinks is best, which is to protect you from harm. It looks behind you and ahead of you and advises you to escape. In its efforts to ease your pain, it will also sidetrack you away from your 'growth priorities'. You'll find yourself engaging in distractions like computer games and the TV, or returning frequently to the fridge or pantry to alleviate stress.

The risk with Depression is that it can have the same effect as an addiction. It will help you avoid what seems to be a very frightening situation; then it rewards you with a message that it saved you the trouble or pain of that situation. More challenges arise and every time you turn to your 'ally' to save you, it finds more escapes and appears to move the difficulties out of your way. The danger, though, is that over time you begin to lose touch with the rest of your surroundings. You don't know it, but you are being robbed of experiences that would otherwise lead to growth and development.

Sometimes, as in my case, retreating leaves the depressed person so trapped and isolated that he or she is no longer able to function. Every time I wanted to do something enjoyable, I would be dogged by the fear of making mistakes or by anxiety about challenging situations. These fears prevented me from navigating my life to include new adventures, new goals, new experiences and new friendships. Instead, I kept trying to control my current experiences and I resisted new experiences that would have helped me to grow and mature.

But that Depressed voice has a counterpart whose perspective is much wiser and more useful. Instead of whispering, 'Retreat!' it whispers, 'Live! Trust! Engage! Be strong!'

The Wise Little Voice has power. It is from the creative part of your mind. It fills you with hope. And with hope, you begin to plan. Your plan turns into a vision. Vision and hope give you the energy to act. With hope, energy and action you are much more likely to realise your vision. As you achieve success in one area, you begin to feel excited about repeating that success in other areas. Over time your success will compound and you will find that your life is beginning to look and feel and sound like your vision.

In the next chapter I share with you the destructive rules by which I'd been living.

EMERGENCY AND SUPPORT INFORMATION

According to Science Daily, 'Depression affects 121 million people worldwide. It can affect a person's ability to work or form relationships, and can destroy their quality of life. In its most severe form, depression can lead to suicide and is responsible for 850,000 deaths every year.' [2]

A summary of an article from Walters Kluwer Health stated: 'About 2.6 million American children and adolescents had diagnosed anxiety and/or depression in 2011-12, reports an analysis of nationwide data.' In other words, more than 1 in 20 U.S. children and teens have anxiety or depression in the U.S. alone. [3]

If you are contemplating suicide and feel you cannot trust any family member or friend with what is troubling you, I urge you to contact the 'emotional emergency helpline' in your country. Here's an international resource for you to quickly find the relevant numbers: *https://en.wikipedia.org/wiki/List_of_suicide_crisis_lines*

In Australia try the following:

- Emergency: 000
- Lifeline Australia: 13 11 14
- Beyond Blue: 1300 224 636
- Kids Helpline: 1800 55 1800
- Confidential Helpline: 1800 737 732
- Mensline: 1300 78 99 78
- Relationships Australia: 1300 364 277
- 000 is the national emergency number in Australia.

---

[2] Source: BioMed Central; article dated July 26, 2011
[3] Source: Wolters Kluwer Health, April 24, 2018

- Lifeline (https://www.lifeline.org.au/) is a 24-hour nationwide service that provides access to crisis support, suicide prevention and mental health support services. It can be reached on 13 11 14. They also offer an online chat service.

- Kids Helpline (https://kidshelpline.com.au/) is a 24-hour nationwide service that provides access to crisis support, suicide prevention and counselling services for Australians aged 5–25. It can be reached on 1800 55 1800. The Kids Helpline also provides online chat services.

- Beyond Blue (https://www.beyondblue.org.au) provides nationwide information and support regarding anxiety, depression, and suicide. It has a helpline which can be reached by calling 1300 22 4636. The helpline is available 24 hours a day, 7 days a week. In addition, the organisation provides online chat (IM) for ages 15 to 24.[4]

If you feel you are in danger of spiralling out of control with depression, anxiety, or any other mental health issue, contacting one of these organisations is one of the most courageous moves you can make. It will most likely turn your life around.

Don't worry about how you are going to sound or what you are going to say. All you need to do is pick up the phone. They will do the work for you. (I could very well have used a service like this if it had been available back in the 80s.)

Today mental health is treated with the same seriousness as physical disease and trauma, and there are many professionals who are well trained in this field and will treat you with the utmost respect.

---

4 Thanks to Wikipedia for this information.

If you are feeling desperate and need to talk to someone, the steps are:

1. Recognise that you need support.

2. Pick up the phone, or at the very least, research which support organisations are available to you.

3. When you have acted upon contacting a professional, congratulate yourself for your courage.

4. When you feel you are ready, find a close family member or friend who you feel can support you as you take action to either treat or overcome your issue. There is nothing like having support during tough times.

After reading this article I wondered if the 121 million people affected by depression were all directly suffering or if that number included the various friends and relatives who experience the effects of depression as a result of their close friends, family and colleagues suffering. Remember that I became depressed as a result of the 'downward emotional spiral' my parents experienced.

There is a significant amount of 'collateral damage'. If you are supporting someone with depression, thank you. Hang in there. You could be providing the lifeline they need for climbing out of the hole they are in.

In a nutshell, here is the strategy I used to avoid suicide. There are many other possible strategies; this is simply what worked for me.

1. Pause. Think. What will happen if your suicide attempt fails but you are irreversibly injured? Imagine lying in hospital with brain damage or stuck for the rest of your life in a wheelchair...

2. Ask yourself: Can *you* possibly benefit from your death?

3. Ask yourself – be honest – how you can be more influential or loved: by dying or by living through this crisis?

4. Find a more creative, inspiring, useful way to 'get vengeance' on others or on life that doesn't cause anyone harm.

5. Trust that your solutions are all inside you.

6. Decide to find a group of people who genuinely respect, like, and appreciate you.

If you want help with depression (or another uncomfortable emotion), here is an exercise for you to do:

In your notebook write down the uncomfortable emotion you are feeling. If there are several emotions, list them all in a column on the left-hand side of your page. Then put your imagination to work and write the complete opposite of each undesired emotion in a column down the right hand-side of your page.

Naming emotions helps to 'divide and conquer' muddled feelings, and identifying the opposite helps you to take a first step in a more useful direction.

As I was able to coach myself out of depression and near suicide, I feel that I have a purpose to help others. I want the 12-year-old version of me to count for something after all the suffering he endured. You can help that 12-year-old version of me, and any family member, friend, colleague or even a stranger you feel is in danger of suicide or depression, by pointing them in the direction of this book.

While I continued to struggle with depression, things steadily got better. Keep reading to find out how I began to ReWrite the Rules of my life.

"The past is your lesson. The present is your gift. The future is your motivation."

– ZIG ZIGLAR

"If you think you will lose, you are lost. For out of the world we find, success begins with a fellow's will… It's all in the state of mind."

– BRUCE LEE

"The key to growth is the introduction of higher dimensions of consciousness into our awareness."

– LAO TZU

CHAPTER 3: The Destructive Rules I Was Living By

"We never know the worth of water till the well is dry."

– 18TH CENTURY ENGLISH PROVERB

On 25 August 1988, as soon as I asked myself the question *'What am I going to do?'* I realised that I needed to change the rules I was living by. My life was in a downward spiral – my self-worth, self-confidence and energy were going down the sewer. I felt I had been mysteriously cursed but actually it was simply a case of a debilitating set of rules. I had no chance of a happy successful life if the rules governing my life were undermining me. And they were undermining me.

There are a certain number of beliefs and experiences that we absorb unconsciously as a result of our parenting and childhood experiences. That's natural. As we mature we make more conscious, responsible choices, but in some areas of our lives many of us continue to be affected by childhood impressions and programming. In my case, I could have observed that other people behaved differently and weren't subject to the same rules as me, but I didn't. I was locked into my perception of life, and by stubbornly sticking to the same set of rules, I perpetuated the same results.

A rule is 'a set of principles governing conduct'. After the 'Little Voice' saved my life, I made myself think about my life honestly, and realised I was living by this very destructive set of rules:

RULE #1: Follow the rules – parents' rules, school rules… Conform. Do what I'm told. Try to fit in.

RULE #2: Believe I'm unworthy. Put my power outside of myself, put it instead in other people. Live at the effect of their opinion of me. Take their taunts personally. Believe their judgemental views of me are right and are the whole truth about me. Be suspicious and nervous of every little facial expression and movement others make, taking them all personally as being about me.

RULE #3: Be resentful of anything that isn't going my way. Believe that life isn't fair.

RULE #4: Expect others to dominate me. Expect to be bullied. Respond by playing victim.

RULE #5: Decide that it's all too hard. Stop trying. Get upset when people tell me to lift my game.

These rules were how I was unconsciously perpetuating an unhappy life. I decided to take responsibility for my life and I've managed to ReWrite the Rules of my life to suit me. In the following chapters I will outline the new rules I devised for myself and explain how I managed to exchange the destructive set for a new constructive set.

Meanwhile I suggest that you now identify the rules that are governing your life. Look at the way you live your life and interact with others and see if you can discover the rules you are currently living by. As we usually make those rules unconsciously, it might not be easy to identify them. The best way is to observe how you are *actually* living and, in particular, how you respond to trouble and challenges. Your beliefs about life are a good clue as to what your rules are. They are your personal code of behaviour.

Make a list of the rules you are currently living by in your notebook.

If we take the time to observe the rules we seem to be living by, we are one step closer to freeing ourselves from the destructive ones. Now choose: Do you *want* to live by those rules? What kind of life are they creating for you? If you don't like the effects of those rules, what kinds of rules do you *want* to live by?

List the rules you would rather live by in your notebook.

"When you want to give up just think of the people who would love to see you fail. DON'T GIVE THEM THAT PLEASURE!"

– UNKNOWN

"Not everyone will make it to your future. Some people are just passing through to teach you lessons in life."

– UNKNOWN

CHAPTER 4: My New Rules, And How I Arrived At Them

> "Sometimes the bad things that happen in our lives put us directly on the path to the best things that will ever happen to us."
>
> – NICOLE REED

> "The secret of change is to focus all of your energy, not on fighting the old, but on building the new."
>
> – SOCRATES

So what were the rules I created that formed the basis of the new David Gillman? At the age of 12 I wasn't sufficiently aware to rewrite all the rules in one go, but I did need a game-changer. As it happens, I made two simple decisions that day, after returning the gun to the gun case, that made a huge difference in my life from then on:

The First Rule

From a young age I had believed that if I did the right things I would 'fit in' and be appropriately rewarded. So when I was told or ordered to study, I would try to study. If told to go to the end of the line when playing house sports, I would go to the end of the line. When my parents told me to turn the TV off and go to bed, I would turn the TV off and go to bed...

But my frustration, anger, and new-found determination drove a decision to stop trying to fit in. *I would become a nonconformist, quietly pursuing my own interests while appearing to conform to the outside world.* This idea cast a magic spell on my young mind. I would make up my own rules! I would set out to achieve my goals with little regard for others who might be trying to compete with me. I was no longer going to operate on other people's terms, unless that competition also served my personal values and desires!

Nonconformity didn't mean that I was no longer going to submit homework or study to the best of my ability (even though most subjects bored me). I wasn't about to start disobeying school rules willy-nilly, and I was still quite prepared to be a team player (if I was miraculously requested to join a team), but if rejected or badly treated, then I was out for myself!

The Second Rule

The other decision that began to turn the tide for me was a resolution to reconnect with old friends. By comparison with my school years, I had happy memories of my first social experiences at kindergarten and prep. About half of those old companions were at my school and even though we had drifted apart, we were not at each other's throats and we had something in common: a shared history.

I stopped pacing around my bedroom and looked out the window again. I stared out at the park that was now bathed in warm, golden sunlight. For a few moments, I conjured a vision. I saw four of us kicking a football to each other, jumping after cricket balls and riding around on our bikes – my vision of happiness.

"I will find them again!" I promised myself. "I will find and reconnect with all my kindergarten friends no matter how long it takes, even if it's after we finish our final year. I will find them and rekindle our friendships. I may be the victim of a curse today, but I'll be buggered if I'm going to have this dictate the rest of my life!"

That was my starting point. I couldn't resolve anything else during that turning-point day as my mind was just too tired to contemplate my other problems. But to me, those decisions were enough for now. For some reason, my spirit began to feel hope.

From that point forward, I put myself on a mission though I never spoke openly about it to anyone. I became a one-man resistance movement! My aim was to revive my happiness by doing the two things that felt good to me at that time: be a nonconformist and resurrect my friendships from the past. My plan might not have had the punch of an army but my resistance movement could conduct secret operations that had its members growing daily, and right under the noses of the authorities – I mean, bullies.

The next day, August 26, I set about reconnecting with a friend from the kindergarten era. That friendship has held firm to this day, and so have the others that followed.

In the years that followed I thought about it all much more and came up with a whole new set of useful rules. If I'd collected them all on one sheet of paper that day when I was 12, here is how they would have read:

Dave Gillman's New Empowering Rules

RULE #1: Instead of meekly going along with everything I will look for ways to express myself, stand out, and be a nonconformist!

Since I was often rejected from sporting teams, I didn't enjoy sport as much as I might have. But during the years of 1987 and 1988, the school librarian started a chess tournament. I had been learning to play for a while and figured that if I could win in my year group, the other students might take note and give me more respect. At least this game was fair and square and nobody could kick me off a team! Instead, my fellow students would have to beat me to be rid of me.

It turned out that the game of chess enabled my creative skills and strategic planning skills to develop. I did win in my year during 1987 and was a runner-up in 1988. Playing chess also gave me the opportunity to fulfil my intention to be a nonconformist since it wasn't a popular interest or activity among most of the kids my age.

My interest in history was also beginning to feature. With the help of my father, I made memorable displays of the projects I was assigned. No other student (to my knowledge) brought in such highly detailed models. (I did the paperwork on these assignments but Dad helped me with the constructions.) I can still remember the bemused looks on the faces of my History and Form Teachers as Dad and I laboriously carried in a hefty 25-kilogram concrete castle, the surrounds of it covered with Plaster of Paris, plastic farm animals, grass and trees glued into the chipboard. It may have been overkill for Year 6 and 7 projects, but I wanted to stand out in the eyes of my teachers and students.

RULE #2: I will find my past friends, those who share a happier history with me, and I will choose new friends who share similar values.

My desire to resurrect kindergarten friendships had been triggered by memories of socialising that weren't sullied by bullying and other school dynamics. (Being 12, kindergarten wasn't that long ago.)

RULE #3: I will not spread ugly rumours about other students. I will do everything I can to avoid a fight, but if unfairly picked on for one and I can't win on the day, I will wait six months and then get them back – on my terms! It's time to frighten those pricks off! Make sure I tell them why I did it as I leave their crippled arses on the ground! Warn them not to come back! I will find a smart way to frighten these bullies so much that they'll never want to mess with me again!

Remember: that was my 12-year-old-self speaking. This rule was by no means perfect and, as I explain in Chapter 6, it nearly led to my demise and the demise of someone else.

RULE #4: I need access to an older generation – people I can trust, people I can confide in; maybe someone who has strategies I can use to keep me safe and sane.

All I had at the time was my parents (whenever they were home) and my grandmother who lived close by and provided a weekend refuge. (I was also soon to have a new Headmaster and Year 8 Co-ordinator who would both look after me.)

RULE #5: I will find out what really excites me in life!

Maybe it's playing chess competitively? Maybe flying a radio-controlled aircraft at school? Maybe clay target shooting? This was where my desire and decision to be a nonconformist really kicked in!

RULE #6: I will learn from the history books!

I will actively apply what I learn in books and films to my own life and head off problems rather than having to learn lessons the hard way through experience! (This was ambitious for me, but not out of reach.)

I really had to dig deep into my character to come up with those new rules. They were not perfect from an adult point of view, perhaps, but they provided a starting point. More importantly, they fed my spirit.

Whenever we are faced with a significant life challenge, nourishing the spirit by meeting our personal needs is an important first step. During our lives we will naturally evolve our rules as our character matures; those rules were my starting point.

We had classic war movies in our home library with titles such as *The Battle of Britain*, *The Battle of Midway*, *The Battle of the Bulge*, *The Blue Max*, *Hornblower* and *Captain Blood*. To be sure, most titles were Hollywood fiction but some were based on true events. To me, they were all inspirational stories. Since I perceived myself to be in a war, I was drawn to watch these films. As I watched them, I found myself searching for ways of my own that I could fight back.

I relived certain moments from those movies over and over again over the course of days and weeks, months and years. I needed a release of bottled-up tension and this was how I did it. Certain scenes would remind me of my situation and so I would apply the film solution. Sometimes a main character would utter a wicked line at a crucial moment, and I knew I could use that line too.

There is an NLP technique called anchoring that consists of associating an emotion with some other dynamic, whether a specific movement or a piece of music or a location. You've probably seen sportspeople make a fist in the air when they score – that's an anchor. Every time they make that fist, they are 'energising' the feeling of triumph. I used movie scores to create anchors. The soundtracks composed by Sir William Walton and Ron Goodwin for the movie *The Battle of Britain* were powerful enough to lift me out of any funk. Movies like this enabled me to embrace hours of isolation after school and on weekends; in the process, I was developing my character for the years to come.

Having searched for answers from the outside for years, my 'Wise Little Voice' had demonstrated that my answers came from within, and it had more good advice for me.

"Five things to quit right now…

    1) Trying to please everyone

    2) Fearing change

    3) Living in the past

    4) Putting yourself down

    5) Overthinking."

— UNKNOWN

CHAPTER 5: Another New Rule: Listen To The Most Empowering Voice

"The starting point of all achievement is desire."

– NAPOLEON HILL

What was to happen next? Would I turn my life around in one clean step or would I continue to struggle and fall and pick myself up again? Or, worse, would I fail again and again to realise my dreams of a better, happier future?

My old rule of trying to fit in with everyone around me was hurting me and I wasn't yet reaping the benefit of the corresponding new rule of being a nonconformist. Trying to please people over the previous few years had left me exhausted, distracted and powerless. At times, in order to win friends and be popular, I had entertained others at my expense. I had no prior successful experiences to draw upon for dealing with my emotions, in particular, the feeling of depression.

But the little voice that had saved me from pulling the trigger became my mentor. It began to instruct me, speaking to me every day. The first thing it advised me to do was to list my problems. So, at the age of 12, I sat at the desk in my bedroom and wrote the following in my exercise book:

1. I'm lonely. I have only one friend.
2. I'm struggling at school. I'm not interested in my subjects.
3. The school sports captains only choose popular students for teams and they always leave me out.
4. I can't seem to stand out from the crowd. I feel unnoticed.
5. I'm heartbroken that the girl I have loved since kindergarten is no longer interested in me. She's got another boyfriend, and he happens to be the guy I am having the most trouble with.

What my little voice did next was to instruct me to create a list of new 'wants'. What I came up with looked like this:

1. I want more friends.
2. I want to enjoy school.
3. I want to be able to compete in a sport in which I decide where my place is!
4. I want to stand out, be noticed for a unique talent.
5. I want to at least be friends with Jo again.

Where did the resources to turn my life around come from? That little voice... and my Dad. As you can see, I was developing another new rule, the rule of consciously and deliberately choosing which voice I listened to: the depressed voice that made me feel down and alone, or a wiser voice, whether it was the inner voice of my intuition or the outer voice of my father.

I swallowed my pride and approached my Dad one night with my list of 'wants'. I didn't tell him about my suicide attempt but I did point out to him some of the reasons I was struggling. (Not 'the girl problem' – I wasn't ready to share that yet.)

Dad listened to my tale and then offered two pieces of advice that aligned spookily with my own ideas. His first comment was: "I think at this stage, Dave, don't worry about playing sport at school."

"Why not?"

"The school doesn't pay you to break your bones or injure yourself. It just uses you for its glory. Even if your team wins in a season, all that happens is that you're quickly forgotten and replaced by another team."

I pondered that for a moment. "What should I do then?"

"You have a shooter's licence. I'll take you clay target shooting on any weekend you're free. That way you can train and compete in a sport that no-one else can arbitrarily kick you out of."

His answer made a lot of sense and aligned perfectly with my instinct. It reinforced my feeling that I was a mug trying to run myself into the ground training for a school sport and team that didn't want me. I began to feel a spark of hope.

"It seems to me, David," Dad added, "that you need to bypass these situations and create your own. Why don't you start inviting kids you used to get along with to visit here instead of waiting for them to approach you? You were so happy at kindergarten and I haven't seen you that happy since then. How many of those friends are still in your year?"

Once again Dad had put his finger on one of the core issues. There were at least six, not including my kindergarten crush, Jo. I knew exactly who I'd start with.

"Now, David, about your marks," Dad continued. "I'm not sure what we can do about those. You do need to start upping your game here."

"Dad, I'm trying but it's so damned hard! The only thing I'm doing really well at is History. No-one can rival me there!"

Having a great deal of knowledge of history at my age did give me a sense of empowerment, and I was deliberately learning from mistakes of the past (the war stories I read and watched) to save myself pain in the future. But as far as I was concerned, I was already 'damaged goods'.

My self-talk had been working against me for so long that I was still largely in its spell. I slugged on because I was convinced that I needed reasonable marks for life after school but the environment I was in was really getting me down, so the next thing I said was: "I wish I could start over at a different school, Dad."

"I don't think that starting at another school will help you, David," he replied.

"Why not?"

"You're very likely to come across similar problems at another school. Running away from one school to another won't solve all your problems."

I nodded but said nothing. What was the point? I thought one thing, and Dad thought something else. We would probably never agree.

"Dave, you're changing campuses next year when you go into high school. You'll have new teachers looking after you then, right?"

"Yes, I guess so."

"Well, just hold on a few more months. Next year you'll have a different headmaster and different teachers and there will be new kids in your classes. It might be a very different year."

I agreed to hold on. I was still gloomy but decided it was easier placing my faith in a more experienced perspective. I kept on at school and survived by burying myself in a field of history that I really related to: World War II Aviation. One day, during a lunchbreak, I was hiding away in the school library reading a book on the U.S. Navy when I came across the recount of an aerial battle that occurred during the Battle of the Coral Sea.

A pilot by the name of Stanley 'Swede' Vejtasa was leading a patrol of 'Douglas Dauntless' dive-bombers in the airspace over his aircraft carrier. Ten minutes into his flight, his squadron was attacked from above by nine Japanese Zero fighters. The U.S. Navy dive-bombers weren't designed for an all-out brawl with the Japanese fighter, and in the following moments of being 'bounced', Swede found himself in a very difficult situation.

Even though he had called out over his radio to break formation, four of his fellow crews were already on fire and spinning out of control. Swede, however, kept his cool. During the course of 19 minutes, he turned his dive-bomber onto three other Japanese fighters. Even though his bomber was armed with a pair of .30 calibre machine guns to the rear of his cockpit, he knew that it was virtual suicide to rely on his rear gunner to defeat his attackers.

In sharp, violent moves, Swede kept turning his aircraft on its wingtips, at times pulling nine times his body weight in G-forces and then suddenly throwing his aircraft into negative G-force manoeuvres. His strategy was to force the three Japanese fighters into tight turns and cause them to eventually make a mistake.

Sure enough, the strategy and the manoeuvring tactics worked. The fight took over twenty minutes, but Swede shot down two aircraft with his nose-mounted .50 calibre machine guns. The final Japanese pilot tried to ram the U.S. naval pilot's bomber in an act of suicidal desperation. At the last minute, Swede jinked his aircraft onto its wingtip, avoiding the head-on collision. The Zero's port wing clipped the wing of Swede's dive-bomber, catastrophically ripping the Japanese pilot's wing. Swede's aircraft survived the collision because it was built of stronger materials. Recovering from the deafening clatter of the collision, Swede turned to see his last attacker falling away and trailing heavy smoke.

He returned to his carrier with his aircraft punctured with bullet holes and a damaged wing, but mainly intact. He was awarded the Navy Cross for his actions and transferred to a fighter squadron where his talents would be fully realised.

I loved reading these pages. Swede was a very skilled pilot and at that time he was up against some of the best trained Japanese fighter pilots in the world. To survive this battle of endurance and skill, outgunned and outnumbered in an aircraft not really suited to aerial dogfighting, and return safe and victorious was a feat of endurance that inspired me to fight on in my own war. Like Swede, I was in a war of endurance. The main thing was to survive until the end of Year 7.

Year 7 didn't finish quickly enough. I still remember walking out though the old black iron mesh gates on the last day at my primary school. I felt as if I was leaving a prison camp.

I spent most of my holidays in my bedroom, playing my Commodore 64. Computer games were my main mental escape from the reality that I was once again to face during Year 8 at my secondary school.

The beginning of the new school year came much too quickly but I rekindled one more kindergarten friendship so I at least now had two friends to hang out with during the morning and lunch breaks. Nonetheless, I continued to struggle at my new school. I never smoked or took drugs to deal with the challenges I faced, but I continued to be bullied and I still couldn't raise interest in my subjects.

However the more I changed my focus from resentment to what I wanted from life, the more I gained a sense of purpose. My focus was changed because I was beginning to rewrite the rules of my life. I had a new mindset that didn't allow anxiety to take over as it had when I was 12. I held on. And by the time I left school, I was able to tick all the boxes of my five 'wants':

1. I want more friends.

My kindergarten friendships eventually grew from two to ten, and we continued to reconnect even after leaving school. (Later in this book, I will share how goal #5 was realised – 'I want to at least be friends with Jo again' –

which was something that I couldn't even dream of during the despairing days of Year 7.)

2. I want to enjoy school.

Meeting with the new teachers, I felt frightened but determined to push on. But I discovered that the new headmaster was a kind, gentle, humane man who genuinely cared for his students. This realisation was something of a shock for me after my previous experience of a stern almost unstable headmaster. Mr John Weedon challenged my belief that all headmasters were strict and scary.

3. I want to be included in school sports.

After speaking to my father, this goal had evolved into achieving success in one of my preferred sports, and one that didn't make me dependent on being chosen for a team. Over time, I became quite a good clay target shooter. After leaving school, I even travelled overseas twice to compete at 'The Grand American' in Ohio where I made some great, long-lasting friendships. These achievements were in stark contrast to those of others in my year who were still reliant on being picked to play on local sporting teams, or even being forced to stop playing sport because of study and work commitments. I am forever grateful to my father for this insight and advice. It enabled me to achieve another of my goals:

4. I want to stand out, to be noticed for a unique talent.

After leaving school I joined the family business since it required another printer. Here I also excelled. Not only was I one of only ten printers in the world who embossed foil lettering on sashes and ribbons, but I became quite proficient with computer graphics and 3D pantograph engraving, which involves the creation of new press badge designs. To my current knowledge, I am the only one in the world capable of all three types of design.

If you take away only one point from this book, take this one: you have both an empowering and a disempowering internal voice, and around you there are both empowering and disempowering external voices. But you can choose which voice you listen to.

OLD DISEMPOWERING RULE #6: Listen to (and believe) my negative self-talk. Listen to and believe the critical comments of others.

NEW EMPOWERING RULE #7: Choose which voice I listen to. Listen to the Most Empowering Voice, whether internal or external.

"The reason people awaken is because they have finally stopped agreeing to things that insult their soul."

– UNKNOWN

"The future belongs to those who believe in the beauty of their dreams."

– ELEANOR ROOSEVELT

CHAPTER 6: Old Rule: Survive!

"Aggressive people have plenty of 'pushing power' but very little 'pulling power.'"

– P.K. SHAW

Some time around the end of 1988 I discovered a war movie recreation of the surprise attack on Pearl Harbor in December 1941. *Tora! Tora! Tora!* quite faithfully represents both sides of this unfortunate event. I'd initially thought that the Japanese attacked the U.S. without delivering a formal declaration of war but I learnt from this film that the Japanese ambassador, through no fault of his own, was delayed in delivering the declaration of war until after the attack was over.

I was fascinated by this movie and watched it over and over again. It resonated with me because to my mind I was under attack. I might have resisted suicide when I was 12 but I had nonetheless formed the belief that war had been declared on me and I hadn't deserved it. I hadn't been asking for trouble, but the bullying that had begun at primary school had continued into my secondary school years.

War movies and books about battles won and lost on strategy and tactics were my launching point for survival and self-defence. I read the Dicta Boelcke, which was a list of fundamental aerial manoeuvres for combat that were formulated by First World War flying ace Oswald Boelcke. I wanted to transform the knowledge from these rules into my own conduct at school. I also wanted to convey a character who couldn't be messed with; Hollywood made dogfights look cool and I hoped some of that cool might rub off on me... I might not have been very successful in this endeavour, but at least those films and books enabled me to develop the grit to come through those hard times.

During the course of those years, as my frustration gave way to action, I began to develop strategies to either deter repeat offenders or to help me at least get through these troubling times. I want to save you as much pain and exhaustion as possible on your journey, so learn from my mistakes as I share with you some of the strategies I implemented during the first 10 of those years. The general rule here was: 'Survive!'

1986: Strategy #1: Call On Superior Powers

In 1986, when I was in Year 5, the bullying got to a stage where I was really struggling to keep my sanity together. At any point in the week ten fellow students were causing me mischief beyond what I could tolerate.

Finally I approached my dad and told him what was going on. He contemplated for a few minutes then brought out a piece of paper and started writing a letter to the headmaster. In it, he described not only my injuries, but the cost of those injuries to my education and general wellbeing, and the financial cost to him as a customer shelling out thousands of dollars a year at a prestigious school and receiving, in return, a compromised service.

About two days later, in the middle of an English class, the headmaster entered our classroom unannounced and called those boys out. I pretended to know nothing as they trailed out of the room. I remember the other students whispering to each other, wondering what was going on.

Twenty minutes later the boys returned, and every boy who walked in came past me and simply said, "Hi David." "Hi David." "Hi David." It was their way of apologising to me without having to say sorry.

When an aggressor is ambushed from an unexpected quarter, it can be extremely humiliating, especially when those aggressors are obliged to acknowledge you in front of their peers. I was left alone for the rest of the year, but this strategy of calling on a 'superior power' had limited power; the following year it all started up again.

1987: Strategy #2: Stand Up For Yourself

One young teenager, quite a bit taller than me, began making a habit of pushing me around in art class. Once again, figuring that getting into a full-on fist fight with him wasn't going to end well, I approached my dad, who was fast becoming one of my most reliable sources of advice. I'll never forget that night as we stood at the kitchen while he was peeling potatoes at the sink.

Dad listened to my plight. He then said, "Son, I think this time you will have to make a stand. The effect of writing letters over and over will be diluted very quickly."

"But Dad, if I fight him I will most likely lose." I hated being hurt – who doesn't?

"Dave, sooner or later you must learn to stand up for yourself."

"If I fight this guy and we're caught, it will be detention. I don't see why I should have to pay double for this!"

"David, I don't have any other ideas here. I think your best strategy is to call him for a fight next time he pushes you. Challenge him to fight outside the front gate of your school during pick-up time."

"But Dad, we'll be caught and that will mean a Saturday detention!"

"That's right."

"What good is that going to be?"

"If you're caught, both of you will be marched into the office and punished with detention. Better serve a detention on Saturday for three hours and take this kid with you than going through these attacks every week."

I paused a moment. My antagonist, 'Darren', had nearly pushed me head first into the side of a bench the previous day. I was only just able to save my balance in time. Still… "But Dad, this is so unfair! You want me to break the school rules and get myself into trouble when I've done nothing wrong?"

"Are the school rules working for you at the moment?" Dad looked at me sternly, but I could see that he was worried.

"I guess not."

"Son, when cornered during the Second World War, the Japanese soldiers would put themselves into a state that made them nearly fearless about their impending doom. They would program themselves to take out as many allied soldiers as they could before the inevitable. You need to deter this Darren from fighting you again."

As ever, the military example clinched it for me.

Things came to a head three days later. I wasn't looking for a fight, but Darren stuck an elbow in my ribs as he passed behind me. I turned around and made my challenge. He accepted. What else could he do? His friends were watching.

I was nervous the rest of the day. I marched out through the school gates at 3:15. Within five minutes, Darren's friends had pointed me out to him. He walked over with his entourage following, dumped his bag and said, "Right! Come on, Gillies! You want a fight? Come on!"

The fight lasted about one minute. Darren got more punches into me than I got into him, but that was to be expected. I just had to hold him off until a teacher arrived. The cheering and jeering of the students surrounding us in front of the school was loud enough to be heard about 20 metres down the road. Mr Grant, the teacher on duty, stormed out of nowhere. He grabbed both of us by the scruffs of our necks and dragged us into the headmaster's office.

The headmaster acted exactly as Dad and I had predicted. After interrogating us as to who had started the fight and me trying to explain why I'd felt obliged to act the way I did, our punishment was announced: a Saturday detention, that weekend.

I looked at Darren defiantly. But deep inside I felt that I had betrayed my own principles. There was a lump in my throat and it was hard to catch my breath.

As we walked out, escorted by the supervising teacher, I turned to Darren and said, "So, was it worth pushing me around?"

"Gillies, I have detentions most weeks. I don't care."

I was about to respond with, "Well, how many weekends are we going to have to lose because you can't keep your frigging hands off me?" But I figured it was a waste of breath. This bozo was just too thick to realise how far I was prepared to go to stop this. I decided to wait and see if he'd have another go at me in the following weeks.

At the end of the day, when Dad picked me up, I couldn't hold back my tears. I was so sick of the bullying and what I had done was so against my spirit that it just broke me. To alleviate my pain, Dad took me to see the progress on the trailer for my boat. A local builder was constructing the trailer for me and it was nearly ready. Touching the steel framing gave me a physical reminder that life was not all bad. I was looking forward to Dad being able to tow my boat out to the surrounding rivers and lakes. Dad's strategy in bringing me here had been to change my mood, and it was successful; he was also rewarding me for showing courage in the face of my challenges.

The detention was three hours of study and 20 minutes cleaning up the oval. There was nothing to clean up, but that didn't make it any better. Nonetheless, Darren stopped bothering me after that detention. Maybe I had just proven to be more trouble than I was worth. I'd hoped that the other students would stop bullying me too, but I wasn't that lucky.

The strategy of calling on a power from left field works when we are young and lack skills and resources, but as we grow older we need to rely on ourselves to solve our own problems. The strategy of standing up for ourselves is valid because, as distasteful as fighting might be, sometimes we find ourselves in situations where we are forced to fight – maybe even to save our lives.

Being bullied is a horrible experience and one that most of us face at some time during the course of our lives. Some people consider it to be 'character building', and perhaps it is. I don't advocate fighting any more than bullying, but as coaches, we instruct our clients to use whatever means are necessary to protect themselves should the unthinkable occur.

1990: Strategy #3:Meet The Enemy On My Terms

In keeping with my first strategy of consulting a higher and invested power, I raised the issue of being bullied with my father's second eldest brother.

My uncle had been in quite a few scrapes during his time, but he seemed to always have a way of winning in the end. One of his favourite schooldays strategies was: 'If beaten up in a surprise attack, wait six weeks and then get them back!' My uncle would wait for his moment, sneak up to within metres of the bully when his back was turned, and then charge him. A running jump and side hip-bump would send this bully to the ground. Without waiting, my uncle would then jump on him, get him in a headlock and pound him in the nose until it bled or broke. A variant of this strategy was to get the bully into a headlock with one arm and pull his hair from behind until he cried in agony.

My uncle's view was that if a bully found himself hurt at the hand of a 'lesser' student he would be less likely to go looking for a fight with him afterwards – especially if he had been made to cry. While the bully lay on the ground, winded and bleeding, my uncle would tell him: "That's for what you did to me six weeks ago!" and then walk away.

At the time I was mightily impressed by my uncle's courage because I was sick of being a punching bag and what I most wanted was retribution. I remember asking my uncle: "What if it's a group of bullies that I'm dealing with? What if there are lots of guys attacking me at the same time?" His answer was, "Pick out the ringleader. Don't fight anyone else. If you are ganged up on at a later stage, pick out the ringleader again and make him hurt twice as bad!"

With these words in mind and a few gentle demonstrations under my belt, I was ready. Sure enough, I found myself in such a predicament. On a rainy day, coming back from choir practice on a typical dark winter's afternoon, I found myself standing in a crowded bus full of fellow students. Three students were sharing a seat right next to where I was standing in the aisle. I'm not sure what they were thinking – maybe they were bored or saw me as an easy target – but they started kicking me in the shins. I was so hemmed in by other students that I couldn't move anywhere, so there was no way I could avoid this situation. Figuring that if I did nothing I was going to be limping around for a few days with bruised ankles, I looked around for the ringleader. I guessed he was the one closest to me by the smirk on his face. He was a year younger than me but I can still see him looking up at me as if to say, "What are you going to do about it, wimp!"

I didn't know his name, but I addressed him quite curtly.

"Kid, stop kicking me."

"Shut up!" was the reply.

"I'm serious! Don't kick me again, you little shit!"

"What are you going to do about it?"

"Don't find out!" Those words escaped through gritted teeth.

The three students gave a mocking "Woooo!" response and ramped up their kicking. Being stuck in the crowded aisle, surrounded by them, I couldn't get away. Twenty seconds later, BANG! One of them had got me right in the funny bone near my shin! I didn't know who it was and I didn't care. In a flash of rage I grabbed the ringleader by his hair and began to pick him up, twisting my hand so the intensity of pain would shock him. It did. The sudden attack caused his face to turn white; then he went red around the eyes. In desperation, he grabbed at my hand. With my free hand I raised it in a fist. The boys in the back of the bus, who could see the commotion, were chanting, "Fight! Fight! Fight!"

Just as I was about to break this kid's nose, I felt one arm lock my arm from behind and another two sets of hands pulling me off this student. Neither of this ringleader's friends went to his aid. I'm not sure if they were too shocked or just didn't know what to do. I was pulled away by fellow students in my year.

The commotion was intense enough that all the students on my bus were called out onto the front lawn. Mr Weedon, our headmaster stormed out in front of us and explained that due to the report he had received of the behaviour on the bus, all future choir classes were cancelled. I thought that Mr Weedon was going to pick me out of the crowd and have me severely disciplined for my self-defence actions. But that never happened.

This group of students never bothered me after that day. I guess I had made my point that the bullying had to stop. So the strategy worked well, even though I hadn't followed all my uncle's instructions.

The problem is, I kept repeating it. I didn't get every student back for unkind behaviour such as this, but I did get a few. Unfortunately, like a kid's attraction to a cookie jar, I became attached to the sweet taste of retribution. I didn't go looking for trouble but I found it more and more difficult to restrain myself from vindictive behaviour. Any last willingness I had to conform to school rules was coming to an end *this year!* I had had enough of suffering anxiety and depression because of pent-up frustration from not being able to do anything in my defence without ending up in trouble. I just refused to take it anymore.

I am left to wonder if Mr Weedon knew this when he sat us all down on the grass that day and didn't pull me out in front of the other students to humiliate me. I will never know. Alas, he passed away many years ago and I am unable to ask him if he remembered that day or what might have been going through his mind.

There are times when you're given no alternative but to stand up for yourself. You make a snap decision and charge into action, for better or worse. With my more mature adult awareness I would like to add: Don't judge people too harshly when they lash out because you don't know why they behave as they do. Not everybody has adequate support at home and some have parents, teachers or employers who actively frustrate them or demean them. While this doesn't give them *carte blanche* for poor behaviour, it does help us to be more understanding and compassionate.

A coach once told me that bullying is a very unsavoury and unfortunate experience in life. Unfortunately, it is also a mechanism of personal evolution; at some point during our lives many of us will experience some form of bullying or even bully others because we all experience a range of emotions and we don't always have the maturity to manage those emotions responsibly. Developing the strength to resist lashing out, or to stand up for ourselves, is part of how we grow, and that growth is the purpose of evolution.

The old rule underlying all the strategies in this chapter was: 'Survive!' In the next chapter I outline a strategy that was also driven by desperation and almost had a fatal outcome for me and/or someone else.

OLD DISEMPOWERING RULE #7: Fight to survive!

NEW EMPOWERING RULE #8: Avoid fighting wherever possible but if there is no escaping a fight, a strong beginning can bring it to an end much sooner than my opponent expects.

Sometimes you just have to hang in there, so be in the strongest mental and physical condition you can. If you think you are likely to be picked on frequently, consider enrolling in self-defence classes.

"You may have to fight a battle more than once to win it."

– MARGARET THATCHER

CHAPTER 7: My Pact With The Devil, And How We Both Won

'Before embarking on revenge, you must first prepare two graves.'
– ANCIENT CHINESE PROVERB

When writing my list of new rules I mostly focused on positive strategies, but Number Three was where my pain surfaced:

'I will do everything I can to avoid a fight, but if unfairly picked on for one and I can't win on the day, I will wait six months and then get them back – on my terms! It's time to frighten these pricks off! Make sure I tell them why I did it as I leave their crippled arses on the ground! Warn them not to come back! I will find a smart way to frighten these bullies so much that they'll never want to mess with me again!'

Between 1985 and 1993 the bullying at school continued sporadically. I wasn't looking for trouble, yet it found me. Sometimes I received deprecating comments about my appearance, sometimes I was pushed or shoved against my locker in front of other students, sometimes I was kicked in the shins under my desk. If I was punched or kicked, usually it was in a situation where I'd be at a disadvantage if I tried fighting back.

My response varied. Sometimes I'd let it go. Other times I'd go to a teacher or the headmaster and complain. If I was lucky, the other party might receive a verbal 'slap on the wrist', but rarely were they reprimanded any further than that. Sometimes I would fight back, and the result would be a draw, with neither side being seriously hurt though both sides were definitely bruised.

My most extreme reaction was to set traps for the bullies. I am not proud of my actions, though watching them fall into my traps did feel good at the time.

This ongoing attack/defence dynamic wore me down. I was pushed and shoved around in front of the other students, who egged on the bully or stood by and laughed. Over and over, my faith in justice from the school staff was not vindicated.

Once the bully had released me, I would try to regain my dignity but I'd be feeling angry for the rest of the day, or the week, or the month, or even for years following. My frustration ate away at me, eroding my concentration during study time and when I was doing chores at home. The initial feelings of humiliation and anger inevitably turned into a grudge.

The effect of a grudge is that once someone has affected you in this way, the experience replays in your mind over and over, depleting your energy. The antagonist has won both ways: he has done with you whatever he physically or psychologically set out to do in that moment, and he has also unknowingly undermined you over the long term. He has fulfilled his whim, but the real damage happens over a longer period when you can't stop thinking about the experience. Like a virus, this 'plagued thinking' weakens us. Meanwhile the antagonist seemingly walks free.

I didn't have any access to self-defence techniques and strategies other than the ones my father gave me and a handful of lessons at a local Karate Dojo. The martial arts lessons I did learn were enough to prevent me from being seriously hurt; Dad, however, was excellent at teaching me the art of war in a psychological sense. Unlike a character out of the many war movies I watched for inspiration and encouragement, my father was a real and living role model. The quality he modelled for me was resilience, and he taught this quality indirectly, by example.

Even though he was still recovering from his nervous breakdown after the episode with the false factory inspector, and even when it seemed that we were going to lose 50% of our clientele to that false inspector's business, it was Dad who decided to keep the doors open. My father made several tooling-related decisions that ultimately quadrupled the volume of our products and 'fireproofed' the business from many further losses. Keeping the doors open was financially painful, but a necessary action that ultimately maintained our standard of living, and even improved our lifestyle over time.

While there are many ways of attaining success in life, including strategies both positive and detrimental to others, perhaps ultimate success in life is the ability to achieve victories without hurting anyone else. Sun Tzu, who wrote *The Art of War*, said: '... *Therefore those who win every battle are not really skilful – those who render others' armies helpless without fighting are the best of all.*'

My philosophy borrows elements of karma: if we treat our environment and fellow man or woman in ways that are selfish or hurtful, they will probably stop caring for us and possibly even act to harm us. Sooner or later selfish behaviour 'boomerangs' back to the perpetrator in ways that we may not be able to anticipate or remedy in time.

The opposite aspect of karma also works: aim to help as many people as possible – treat them thoughtfully and caringly because you never know… one day you may be rescued by the very person your previous actions inadvertently assisted. I have been the benefactor of unexpected kindness, or 'good karma', from sources that have left me dumbstruck! Good deeds and selfish deeds affect those around you, and subsequently affect your environment, and even the whole population. Think of them as being like a virus. As with memes on Facebook, we want our positive acts to go viral!

> "When anger rises, think of the consequences."
>
> – CONFUCIUS

1990-1993 Strategy #4: Get Even.

During this period I was required to defend myself against bullying over and over again. My strategies generally improved but one particular incident almost had me undone.

I had come up with a number of responses that varied according to the nature and severity of the actions against me. In most cases I had a three-strike policy: I turned the other cheek three times, but if the bullying behaviour persisted I would retaliate with a very quick, surprise ambush on the perpetrator. No warning, just a short, sudden, and quite alarming attack. I didn't get everyone back but I needed to make it known that I was capable of attacks that were just as uncomfortable as theirs on me.

The problem with my strategy, though, was that I became drunk on revenge, and during my final year at school I was nearly destroyed by an act of vengeance.

By this time I had experienced years of torment at the hands of a fellow student who was, frankly, a thug. Like any thug, he was ever on the hunt for an opportunity to strike out at someone he thought was an easy target. In the movie *Back To The Future* a character called Biff Tannen caused the protagonist, Marty McFly, a lot of trouble. My 'Biff Tannen' character caused me an awful lot of trouble too. I wanted nothing but friendly relations with him, but he was volatile and unapproachable.

One day my volleyball team had won an initial round and the new captain was picking his team. The captain was this Biff character. One by one he called the names of other guys, but not my name. Finally I went up to him and asked if I could play on the team, or at least be considered for interchange. He gave his sardonic grin, and then, with no warning: SHOVE! I was pushed straight onto my backside. I tried to get up but he had a friend with him who shoved me back down with his foot. I tried to get up again and was shoved once more. They both laughed at me then told me to 'F' off.

I felt totally mistreated! Not only was I humiliated, but I was physically hurting. Later it was discovered that my coccyx had been damaged in that first thud to the floor. It took a long time to heal.

This blatant bullying caused me so much frustration that I deliberately plotted Biff's demise. I was so used to getting revenge that I was becoming addicted to the sweet taste and invigorating feeling of justice. It was like a drug. But this fellow was much taller, much more powerful than me. I had to engage him on my terms.

So I waited. The issue sat on the back burner. 1991 turned into 1992. This 'Biff Tannen' had become more popular with fellow students, who turned a blind eye to some of his actions towards easier targets. Another few minor occurrences with him in front of both male and female students finally pushed me over the edge and into action.

One midwinter day I was packing up early in the locker room. I was suffering another bout of depression and couldn't wait to get out of there. As I stowed my stuff in my bag I sensed someone else had arrived. It was 'Biff'. He had his back to me as he concentrated on finding an item in his locker.

I was so worked up by his mere presence that, before I'd realised what I was doing, I'd reached for my hockey stick.

I only need five seconds. Creep up behind... just one crack at his skull, and if it looks like he's going to get up again, just one more.

I wanted to hurt him as he had hurt me. Ironically, I wanted to send him a message about the painful effect of meaningless violence; I wanted to do to him what he had done so often to me. It's amazing how big a blind spot we can have when we are hurting.

The little voice in me that I recognised from my previous suicide attempt seemed to shout at me. *Hey! What do you think will come out of this, you dummy?!*

'Sweet revenge!' I answered silently.

Yeah... sure! So you hammer the crap out of him for all the crap he's done to you. You'll feel better... for about 30 seconds. But if you kill him, then what? What will become of you? The voice was a little sarcastic.

'Peace of mind.'

Yeah... for thirty seconds. Because if you kill him and you're found... On the other hand, if you screw this up, that hockey stick could end up implanted in your skull!

'Maybe,' I replied. I was gripping the stick very tightly at this stage. 'But this jerk needs to be taught a lesson...'

The only lesson that will ultimately come of this is that you could kill him and end up in jail. Do you know what they would do to you in jail? The little voice seemed to hold an invisible hand on my shoulder.

I paused. The answer was obvious. Whichever way it went, my solution of the hockey stick into this fellow's head was going to end in disaster for me.

He'll get his comeuppance, one way or the other! the little voice said in a reassuring tone. *It may not be you directly that gets him; his over-confidence will be his undoing. He might continue to get away with stuff like this for now but eventually it will catch up with him. But if you go to jail, this arsehole wins. You might think that killing him takes out an enemy, but your life becomes more complicated and the memory of him will ruin your future for good!*

I was disarmed. I put the hockey stick in my bag and walked out past 'Biff' without a backward glance.

It turns out that my decision that day *not to act* was significant for the rest of the world.

'Biff Tannen' finished school, studied for a while at university, and then went overseas to pursue his interests. He later attained a high status in the community. He married and had a family. He volunteered for charities and fed and housed many people for free. He became a millionaire. Today he travels all over the world instructing other professionals in his field and has been interviewed by celebrities.

And he is here, doing all of that, because I refrained from knocking him out with a hockey stick during our final years at school.

So here is where I ultimately won: I realised that one indulgent moment of revenge could be the end of me (along with the end of him). My life continued and improved because I allowed reason to penetrate the heat of my upset. And Biff's life continued and improved for the same reason. At one level he may not really owe me anything, but at another this man is enabled to do what he does because of my ability to work through my difficulties – and thanks to the little intuitive voice that was warning and guiding me.

Because I made the decision to leave him alone, charities will continue to receive money and resources from this man's work. He will continue to live his life, pursuing his dreams in relative peace, watching his children grow up and his empire grow stronger. All because I let him live!

So who, in reality, is the winner here? It seems to me that there are many winners: Biff, me, and the world. As far as I'm concerned, I have contributed significantly to the world without having to lift a finger!

The following quote is probably one of the most powerful thoughts I have ever heard. It has guided me through life ever since I first heard it.

> 'Once you start down the dark path, forever will it dominate your destiny… Consume you, it will…'
>
> – YODA

The thirst for vengeance poisons your spirit and robs you of your life, your friends and your family. You don't see its effect until it's too late. You run the risk of robbing yourself of opportunities in careers and alliances that will help you to grow. The effect could be devastating if you seriously injure or kill someone in an act of vengeance.

Most bullies have narcissistic or even sociopathic tendencies – they generally only care about what they want, and they demonstrate little to no sympathy toward the people they affect. The self-absorbed behaviour of the bullies I encountered so confused and frustrated me that *I became equally self-absorbed*. I, too, drifted into behaviours that bordered on narcissism. My decision to fight fire with fire in order to teach this particular bully a lesson was a pact with the devil. I wanted to win or at least get even, and for a few dangerous moments I was prepared to do whatever it took.

It's what we are affected by that we don't understand that has the potential to really confuse and hurt us. Like children watching a magic trick, we see the illusion but not the working mechanics of how it was performed. My self-development studies over the last few years have helped me understand why I acted and reacted the way I did in the past.

In hindsight, what I didn't understand until studying narcissistic bullies was that they are hiding a pain of the past, something that shames them. It may be that a parent or elder siblings are beating them up behind closed doors, or perhaps they are struggling academically. Whatever it is, it leaves them feeling that they have to protect themselves and create a new life, a new social order that they can control, so they will choose the friends and activities where they can reign supreme.

Both 'Biff Tannen' and I had been trying to hide something. I don't know what it was in his case, but in my case it was initially that business-induced stress at home, and all the resultant stresses, including rejection by my peers, my poor marks and my feeling of being uncared about by teachers.

Did my pact work? In sum, the outcome was a stalemate. Trying to fight fire with fire does not guarantee a happy ending for either party.

OLD DISEMPOWERING RULE #8: React! Avenge myself! Block the little voice of my conscience! Get even! Pay back! (This was a survival rule...)

NEW EMPOWERING RULE #9: Think twice before acting in vengeance. When contemplating revenge on anyone, interrupt that pattern by sitting quietly and allowing my mind to coach me to a solution.

Revenge of any type might seem as soothing as scratching an itch, but you can become so used to it that sooner or later you will scratch an area that will infect your life and may drastically complicate your future. If you feel like lashing out, take a few minutes to sit quietly and appeal to your higher intelligence and reasoning instead. Choosing to *not* harm others is much more empowering than choosing to lash out; self-control is a far more impressive ability than reactivity.

Weigh up the pros and cons of reacting in anger, and the pros and cons of finding a better response. Remember that if you act impulsively, the perpetrator will probably still have their way with you and/or you will suffer in some other way. (There are just as many bullies ganging up on other inmates in prison or detention.)

If you succumb to acts of violence, most likely you will end up surrounded by like-minded people who regard your life with very little respect, whereas if you exercise prudence and mercy instead of vengeance you will most likely find yourself surrounded by people with positive, life-affirming values.

If you follow these general principles you have a much better chance of not acting on a grudge. Grudges have consequences that can be so unpredictable that they have a high chance of ruining your life! And since difficult relationships don't stop at school but follow us into our adult lives, learning better skills is very, even critically, important.

General advice for not getting into that sort of situation in the first place!
1. Prevention is better than cure: aim to create a group of like-minded friends so you are less likely to be of interest to those who may wish to amuse themselves at your cost.

2. Talk your way out of an altercation whenever you can.

Disarming a person with words rather than violence is much more favourable to your wellbeing. Keeping in mind that your opponent is most likely angry, getting him or her talking may provide the best means of resolving the issue in a friendly way.

- Practise the following in your mind so that you have a better chance of breaking your opponent's pattern of anger and can instead begin to build rapport.
    - "Why are you angry? Please tell me." OR "I'd like to understand more about why you want…." (Maybe the bully just needs to be heard.)
    - "There might be an easier way to resolve this issue. Let's sit down and discuss this."
- Treat them as if they are intelligent. (You may not believe this about them, but for the sake of avoiding fists and feet flying it may just be worth it.)
- If possible, use a caring tone of voice. Avoid using a tone that sounds either angry or intimidating.

Most importantly, if you get your opponent to talk, shut your mouth and listen. Avoid interrupting them. This doesn't mean that you have to agree with what this person is saying or doing. Let them say their piece. Acknowledging their point of view will go a long way toward placating them, and you may find yourself more easily meeting them halfway than you'd have thought possible.

There are many interesting YouTube videos you can watch on this subject. Typing in the search bar *'How to talk your way out of a fight'* generates many useful pieces of information.

3. Train as early as you can in whichever type of self-defence you relate to.

Walk away from attack whenever you can because there is always the possibility that a physical altercation will not end up the way you hoped it would go. Even if you win you might find yourself walking around with a target on your back because your opponent feels he has unfinished business with you. Not all fights are avoidable but making a genuine attempt at placating your opponent may prove more practical in the long run.

Sometimes that isn't possible. Martial arts should be your last line of defence but some form of self-defence may be useful to have up your sleeve if you have no alternative but to save yourself.

4. Most importantly, create an enriching life for yourself. Don't just dream about it! Act on it. Decide what experiences will enrich your life and pursue them.

In the next chapter I outline the likely outcome had I reacted in violence. The facts described in that 'almost future' were provided or confirmed by a police officer.

"You cannot get through a single day without having an impact on the world around you. What you do makes a difference and you have to decide what kind of difference you want to make."

– JANE GOODALL

"The best revenge is massive success."

– FRANK SINATRA

CHAPTER 8: The Likely Outcome Of Living By The Rule of Violence

> Social justice cannot be attained by violence. Violence kills what it intends to create.
>
> – POPE JOHN PAUL II

What would have happened if I'd lost control of myself and belted Biff with the hockey stick? I met a policeman through my branch of Toastmasters who filled me in. The likely outcome would have been horrifying…

I was nervous when I met with 'Ben' to describe the situation, even though it had occurred over 25 years ago. But he understood my reasons and my aim to save lives by honestly sharing my experiences in this book.

First, Ben asked me to describe what I would have done next if I had taken advantage of us being alone in the locker room and had lashed out with my hockey stick and cracked Biff's skull. I told him that I would probably have stood over a now deceased Biff thinking about how justice had finally been served and my thirst for vengeance had finally been quenched. As this would have been a 'heat of the moment' act, I would have had no plan for what to do next.

Ben described a disturbing image of blood and brain matter staining my hockey stick. As he pointed out the messiness of this sort of attack, it dawned on me that Biff's DNA would have splattered onto my school uniform and shirt too, and I would be in quite a mess.

The immediate problem, though, would have been the hockey stick. Even though it was labelled with my name, I would have been in such a panic that I'd have forgotten that and would have been intent on getting rid of it as soon as possible. I would have had to grab my school bag and hightail it out of the locker area for the other side of the school where, hopefully unnoticed, I could dump the hockey stick in a skip. Somehow I would have to conceal any noticeable mess on my blazer, maybe washing what I could off with an outside garden tap, again hoping no-one would see me.

With no time to hide the body, I would have had to blend back into the crowd of students until the final home bell rang. By the time the bell was rung, the body would have been discovered.

This is when Ben took over and helped draw the rest of the picture for me.

Ben stated that once 000 had been called, the school would have been instructed to shut down the area, and teachers would have been instructed to hold students in class until the police arrived. The main priority of police at that time would be to ensure that other students were not in harm's way. Multiple police units would have been dispatched to the school, including patrol supervisors and crime investigation units. Once the crime scene was located, isolated, and the area declared safe, students would be released from class and the school taken off lockdown.

DNA samples would have been collected from Biff's remains for comparison against any potential suspect's clothing or other evidence. A swift and thorough search of the school by police would soon have located my bloody hockey stick, discarded in the skip. This hockey stick, labelled with my name, would instantly tie me to the incident as a likely suspect. Later, both Biff's and my DNA evidence would have provided the ultimate confirmation.

Ben asked me how he thought I would be feeling by this stage, knowing that police were on the scene. I suspected that I would have been very concerned and on edge. As I had never committed a crime before, the thought of detectives setting their sights on me as their main suspect would have been foremost in my mind. The thought of them knocking on our front door and my puzzled and then disbelieving parents being told of my actions made me feel sick.

Detectives would have spoken with staff members, asking questions about any disputes Biff might have had with other students, whether mild disagreements or fist fights. They'd have asked if anyone was likely to be holding a grudge against him. All lockers would have been opened and searched. As the number of hockey players training at my school was limited, the list of suspects would have been narrowed down very quickly.

Meanwhile, as soon as I got home I would have done my best to secretly bleach my shirt and wash and disinfect my school blazer, hopefully without my parents noticing me. Being a typical teenager, this would have been out of the ordinary behaviour as my mother was the official cleaner in the house. My feelings of tension would have been intense.

I would have had a terrible night's sleep, if any. I would have been concerned that I might have been seen by a student or teacher, especially when I was at the skip, an area I wasn't supposed to be in at that time. I would have lain awake all night worrying about a knock on the front door. A news report may have been presented on the radio or TV that would have alerted my parents to the crime and heightened my anxiety and fear about being caught. It would be highly unlikely that anything negative would have been reported about Biff, the victim.

The next morning, blurry eyed, I would have tried to put on a brave front – difficult to do with bloodshot eyes and after little sleep.

School would have commenced the following day as normal. There may have been no assembly as the teachers would have been instructed not to comment on what had happened until a few days after the initial investigation.

The evidence pointed to someone with access to the hockey equipment, thus all of the players would have been suspected by police. As the day wore on, I would have been dreading the moment I was summoned to the principal's office. Would I be summoned over the loudspeaker? Would the Vice-Principal quietly come in and whisper to my teacher? Or would detectives attend my class?

GULP!!!

Trying to remain composed, though probably feeling slightly nauseous, I would have entered the office to find the headmaster and several detectives waiting for me. Ben indicated that by this stage the evidence against me would be substantial and the detectives would be confident I was the murderer. They may have asked if I knew the victim and if so, how well? Did I have any problems or confrontations with the victim? It wouldn't be long before they asked me where my hockey stick was, to which question I would have replied that I didn't know.

The detectives would then advise that the murder had been traced to a dumped hockey stick found the previous day and that DNA tests were being performed. They would have requested my school uniform for DNA testing, and they would have asked me if I would submit to a warrant for a search of my house for the hockey stick.

I am certain that by this stage I would have cracked. With all the pressure of these questions and the image of my parents' house being torn up by police detectives looking for a murder weapon hockey stick and any stained school clothes, there would have been no way that I would have been able to conceal my guilt.

After my confession, the detectives would declare that I was under arrest. I would be read my rights, my school blazer would be taken as evidence, and the handcuffs would have been applied. My parents would still not know that I had been arrested.

Imagining myself being escorted to the police car with my hands behind my back in cuffs, wondering who was witnessing this walk of shame, and then the ride in the back of a police car to the station, I knew that the weight of my mistake in judgement would be weighing heavily. I would have been feeling deeply embarrassed, knowing that my friends and other students would by then be learning of my fate and Biff's, not to mention all my family members.

The police car, with me in the back seat, would have passed into a secured concrete holding garage. An electric roller door would descend, closing out the outside light.

I would have been escorted to a whitewashed three-metre-by-three-metre custody centre, ordered to strip down to my underwear, given a paper zip suit, and escorted to the interview room where the cuffs would have been taken off. I would sit down at a table with two chairs opposite me. The custody sergeant would arrive and ask me if I knew why I was there.

Meanwhile my parents would be learning that I had been arrested, and would be summoned to the police station. Upon their arrival (with some new clothes for me) they would have been permitted to sit with me prior to the interview. A lawyer would have been called.

It is likely that the lawyer would have suggested that I say nothing further in answer to any questions. The police would again have put their allegations to me relating to the crime. A formal request for a search warrant on my parents' house would have been issued.

At this stage, Ben asked me what would I likely have done: remain silent with no comment in the interview room, or would I have cracked? I know I would have cracked. I would have told the interviewer that I'd had enough after being bullied repeatedly over the course of several years. I'd grown tired of Biff getting away with it and had taken to him with the hockey stick because I wanted justice!

Ben said that at this stage, as I was co-operating with the police and had no prior convictions, I would most likely have been released on bail. However I would have been charged with murder. If I hadn't co-operated with the police, I would have been considered a bully with sociopathic tendencies. In that case, I would have been kept in remand as I would be considered a social risk to others.

Six to eight months later, a court hearing would take place. My lawyer would be given a list of the charges and would advise how best to challenge each charge to the point that it became less severe, such as manslaughter instead of murder.

Given my age, if found guilty I would have been sent to juvenile prison. My prison sentence would be between two and five years (according to the laws in Australia). I would have been sent to prison where I'd have been strip-searched again and then taken to my cell where I would most likely find that my cellmates had the same aggressive characteristics as Biff – and me, as it turned out… If I thought Biff was bad, any one of these inmates could have been a lot worse. Ben mentioned that in many cases, these inmates would mess with a newcomer purely from the need to satisfy their boredom or because of dissatisfaction with their own lives.

This is a sorry tale. Now add on the other costs of bullying.

Consider the victim. Who, really, is the victim here? The bully who was severely beaten or killed? His or her victim who cracked and took matters into their own hands? The family members of both parties? Their friends?

The story wouldn't end with prison; there would have been an even bigger price after leaving prison, a price that would have followed me for the rest of my life. Not only would there have been an enormous cost to my body and soul in terms of physiological and emotional stress, but also in terms of my involvement in the outside world.

According to Ben, with a serious conviction like this on my record I would not be allowed to travel overseas. *Ever again.* Any possibility for future growth and development, fun and adventures would be severely impacted. Not having finished school, I would have struggled for employment opportunities and been reliant solely on the family business for an income. If, for example, I wanted to work outside of the business and become a dance teacher, it would have come through on my application that I had a criminal record, which would have severely impacted my chances of working with the very people I would soon look up to. I would not be allowed to have a Working With Children Check, thus ruling out my ever being able to work with youth. Bank loans and mortgages would be much harder to come by. My firearms licence would have been revoked and I would not have been able to continue with my hobby of clay target shooting.

The financial cost would have been exorbitant as well. The lawyer's fees for my defence would most likely have been paid by my parents, which would have put them under financial strain. The cost on the public purse to cover an investigation of this nature is in the range of $25,000 to $150,000 dollars.

Then there's the psychological impact of the whole experience on my parents. They would have agonised, wondering where they went wrong and what they could have done to prevent this situation from occurring. The impact on any student or teacher who might have found Biff's remains would have been significant. As for me, I would most likely have felt haunted by Biff for the rest of my life.

The following quote from Sun Tzu's *The Art of War* comes to mind: *'Anger can revert to joy, wrath can revert to delight, but a nation destroyed cannot be restored to existence, and the dead cannot be restored to life.'*

What of Biff's family? What would his parents have gone through, knowing that their son wasn't going to be coming home again and the boy who killed him was still alive? Would my prison sentence be enough for them or would they want blood?

The cost of bullying in our times is as staggering as it is complicated. It is both psychologically and financially costly. It is a worldwide ongoing problem.

When I researched the topic of bullying for a short speech at Toastmasters recently, I was stunned by the latest statistics in the United States. The figures in the table below were taken from a 2016 report by the National Center for Education Statistics and indicate the number and percentage distribution of students aged 12 through 18 who reported being bullied at school in 2014-15, by type of bullying.[5]

Type of bullying reported	Estimated number of students	Per cent of students
Bullied	5,041,000	20.8%
Made fun of, called names, or insulted	3,223,000	13.3%
Subject of rumors	2,968,000	12.2%
Threatened with harm	941,000	3.9%
Pushed, shoved, tripped, or spat on	1,235,000	5.1%
Made to do things they did not want to do	607,000	2.5%
Excluded from activities on purpose	1,220,000	5.0%
Property destroyed on purpose	440,000	1.8%
Not bullied	19,202,000	79.2%

Today we also have the problem of cyberbullying. In this case, the student doesn't even need to be at school. Instead, bullies taunt and bait their victims in cyberspace from the safety of their own bedroom computer or smart device.

---

5 SOURCE: U.S. Department of Justice, Bureau of Justice Statistics, School Crime Supplement (SCS - Version 1) to the National Crime Victimization Survey, 2015.

Then there is the issue of how to respond if one is bullied. The ideal response is to act in such a manner that one is no longer an easy target. Unfortunately it is not easy to deter bullies once they have one in their sights.

However when a bully or group of thugs push their victim to breaking point, they may find themselves sitting on a ticking time bomb. My story about Biff isn't the only one.

On the 20 April 1999, 18-year-old Eric Harris and 17-year-old Dylan Klebold, students at Columbine High School, killed 12 students and one teacher. They injured 21 additional people, and three more were injured while attempting to escape the school.

According to Wikipedia, *'Ten minutes after the first shot was fired, Harris and Klebold entered the Columbine school library where a total of 52 students, two teachers and two librarians were trapped and hiding. Harris shouted "Get up!" to the students. "Everyone with white hats, stand up! This is for all the stuff you've given us for the past four years! All jocks stand up! We'll get the guys in white hats!" When nobody stood up, Harris was heard saying "Fine, I'll start shooting anyway!"*

'Approximately 49 minutes after the first shots were fired, the pair committed suicide in the library after a brief gunfight with police at the end of the massacre.

'Their precise motives were unclear, however their personal journals stated that they wanted their act to rival the Oklahoma City bombing. Both students were being treated for depression.

'What was revealed after the massacre, and is understood to be a very important contributing factor, was that both boys had been tormented at school.

'Both of the shooters were classified as gifted children who had allegedly been victims of bullying for four years. According to Brooks Brown, Klebold and Harris were the most ostracized students in the entire school, and even many of those close to them regarded the two as 'the losers of the losers'.

'Klebold is known to have remarked to his father of his hatred of the jock culture at Columbine, adding that Harris in particular had been victimized by this social group. In this remark, Klebold had stated, "They sure give Eric hell."

'On another occasion just weeks before the massacre, both Harris and Klebold had been confronted by a group of youths at the school—all members of the football team—who had sprayed them with ketchup and mustard while referring to the pair as 'faggots' and 'queers'.'

This is just one among many incidents worldwide of the ultimate and most horrifying outcomes of bullying. Many more examples can be found by browsing the Internet today.

Whether the action taken by a victim of bullying is an emotional reaction or a pre-determined decision (such as what happened at Columbine), the victim who turns murderer will most likely experience only one outcome: their own demise.

Those who allow a bully to push them around often end up bullying others and participating in gang-related crimes; at the very least, they develop destructive personal rules. In my case, I was moments away from making a decision to take someone's life because I wanted to satisfy my need for retribution and couldn't stand that I had let this creep get away with what he did for so long!

There was a cost to me of my life energy because so much of my energy was misdirected toward annoyance and frustration, even after leaving school. But as the years went by and time began to heal my coccyx bone as well as my ego, I came to realise that my hesitation with the hockey stick was a very great blessing: I had walked free without a police record interfering with the rest of my life. Instead I have grown, travelled, made friends and contributed to many people's lives, not just in my country, but overseas as well. Above all, I have retained my freedom and autonomy.

I'm grateful to Ben, the patient police officer who ran me through this timeline of what might have happened had I followed through.

So what could I have done to prevent Biff and others from bullying me?

1. Learning and practising some form of martial arts would have been a smart move as it would have given me a means of protecting and defending myself against others' cruelty.

2. Making more of an effort to create friendships with students other than just my close circle of friends would have helped protect me against bullying, not only because I'd have had a bigger support group but because I wouldn't have stood out as such an easy target.
3. Avoiding the areas they haunted would have been wise. In retrospect, I threw myself under the bus too often by hanging out in the bullies' areas.

In the previous chapter I shared the quote, *'Before seeking revenge, first prepare two graves'*. If you are struggling with the need for revenge against a bully, this chapter and the list below will help you realise that revenge is too costly a price to pay for the brief pleasure of gratifying your frustration.

Cost of My Revenge

Respond in detail to the following questions in your notebook.

1. Am I likely to suffer consequences when the law catches up with me?
   If so, what would they be? Might I be arrested? Will I lose friends? Will I lose the trust and respect of family members? How will my health be affected? Will I lose freedoms and privileges, such as overseas travel? (Another risk is to special licences requiring background criminal checks.)
2. Will my parents/guardians suffer from my actions when they don't deserve to? How might they be affected?
3. Is this bully worth so much personal loss and destructive effects on others?
4. How will I feel about this bully or bullies when they are deceased and I am locked up and paying for my act of revenge for the rest of my life?
5. What action can I take right now to prevent this situation from escalating?
6. If uncertain what action to take to avoid this situation, what resources do I have to help me? Counsellors? Life Coaches? Self-defence classes? Who can help me? (There is always someone who cares.)
7. How soon can I contact someone for help, and who will I contact?

By following this checklist, you will have begun to set in place a new and more empowering strategy. Instead of reacting to your environment you will be behaving in a way that is proactive, independent and resourceful. Decide that *you* will determine the direction of your life! Better choices will lead you into a far more fulfilling and prosperous future!

"Mercy is better than justice."

— VAUVENARGUES

CHAPTER 9: New Rule: Hold Onto Your Dreams And Let Go Of Your Illusions

"Those who lose dreaming are lost."

– AUSTRALIAN ABORIGINAL PROVERB

So, okay, I survived school. But what state of mind was I in by the time I left? Had I matured, considering all the mental-and-physical-abuse-baggage I was carrying? What was I to make of my life from age 18 onwards?

I was relieved to be finished with school at the end of Year 12 but I was leaving with my spirit crushed. I had no girlfriend, no self-confidence, and no clear idea of what I wanted to do for a career. I did have a job to go to, in the family business, but initially it didn't inspire me. And I had at least built up a group of school friends, so I was achieving one of my life goals, but no girlfriend. I had also 'saved Biff's life' (although I didn't at that stage know he would go on to make a significant difference in the world), and so, much as I had wanted to make an impact, I felt I was leaving school without achieving that goal (although in retrospect the attention I received for my chess prowess, impressive projects, and flying of radio-controlled aircraft probably did equate to a 'tick' for that item).

My father gave me one week to decide if I was going to start working for him in his printing business in Campbellfield. Since my marks were short of what I needed to enter university or technical college, I reluctantly began work. At the time I wasn't in the right headspace to commence work but I forced myself anyway. I was feeling crushed and disappointed. You could say I'd been living the disempowering rule: *'Give up on your dreams. Don't believe anything special will happen to you. Live a small life.'*

There were, however, some highlights during those first years in the workforce that my regular wage enabled. My interest in shooting saw me competing at the Grand American in Ohio twice – in 1996 and 1999. That first trip in August 1996 represented my debut into the rest of the world.

I left Melbourne during a cold, dark winter and landed in Ohio during their summer. This experience of different climates, the new surrounds and the friendly people made me feel as if I had woken up in the body of a stranger; my unhappy past was nothing but a distant memory that had no relevance to the rich experience I would have over the next two weeks of that first competition.

The Grand American Clay Target Shoot is held over a period of 10 days, and is the most intense clay target shooting event I've ever attended. I was one of about 22 Australian shooters, and found myself tagging along with a close-knit group from Bendigo Clay Target Club. But we were each here on our own merits: we had worked hard, trained hard, and paid for our attendance from our own pockets. There was no popularity contest to stay on the house team; it was every man and woman for themselves.

Presentation of the 97th Grand American Handicap winner sash, 1996

For the first time in my life I was competing in an international event. It dawned on me, as I stood at my station for my first target, that the lessons learned years earlier from competing at the school chess tournament were now standing me in good stead and proving what my father had claimed: it was better to be reliant on myself and not dependent on the choices and decisions of others. I distinctly remember raising the stock of the gun to my cheek and blasting my first target to powdered fragments as it left the trap house.

I didn't win the Grand American Handicap, but I did present the winning sash from our company to a proud winner, Mr Bud Fini, at the presentation ceremony as the representative of my father's business and my country. Did it matter to me that I didn't win? Honestly, no. My personal victory was simply that I had lived long enough to compete at an international level among my peers, and I had walked away with a reasonable personal score and my head held high.

After competing at this event, my return trip was a stopover in Los Angeles where I had one last major dream to fulfil – Disneyland! Ever since I was a child I had wanted to go to Disneyland. I used to dream that this famous amusement park would open up right next door to my house, and all I had to do was run around the side fence at any time and be standing at the entrance. On this occasion, the hotel I was staying at was just across the road.

On the first day, a beautiful sunny afternoon, I walked through the entrance and almost immediately came upon the statues of Walt Disney and Mickey Mouse. It seemed that their eyes were transfixed on me. I still remember walking up to the statues, taking my hat off and quietly conversing with the two figures: 'I made it, guys!' I murmured, not wanting to look too strange to the crowds of people passing by. 'I waited twenty years to do this. I am David Gillman. I've come all the way from Glenroy and Essendon in Melbourne. Thank you for having me here!' It might sound odd that a twenty-year-old would talk to statues of childish icons, but remember that I'd had a lonely embattled childhood and often it had been fantasy characters that kept me going.

Each morning I would wake up, get dressed, grab my water bottle and head over there. I was struck by the positive vibe this place gave me. Every night I would watch the fireworks either from the hotel or from one of the tree houses of the Swiss Family Robinson feature. As I observed the colourful, booming, crackling spectacle, I couldn't help but ponder the struggles of my childhood. When that cold dreadful day in August 1988 reappeared in my mind I was deeply thankful to 12-year-old me for not pulling the trigger. The realisation that I'd grown through that experience and was now alive to realise a childhood dream and discover the world gave me the fuel to carry on and face whatever challenges lay ahead, and the encouragement to experience more of the world. On the last night I made a pact with myself: I would go out into the world and explore the many other great capital cities, townships and countryside the world had to offer.

In keeping with that promise, I travelled to Egypt in 2000 with an old school friend, Rishi. As a child, I would flick through the pictures of a book entitled *The Great Pyramids* that my dad had in his library. I wondered how it would feel to be there, in a country whose history went back over 4,500 years. What would it feel like to look upon the golden sarcophagus of King Tutankhamun or to walk in the halls of the Cairo Museum and behold the ancient mummies of Seti I and Ramses II. After watching the 1956 movie, *The 10 Commandments*, I wanted to interact with the remnants of history. I wanted to experience those places for real!

David at Giza, 2000

I was certainly not disappointed. To this day I joke with my friends that it was so real, it was surreal! The citizens of Cairo, Aswan and Abu Simbel were very warm and welcoming, but of all the temples, mosques, tombs and shops we visited, there was one experience that impacted me so much that I feel it changed my view of spirituality.

It is difficult for me to articulate. It's hard enough to just describe the experience! We were on a guided tour of the pyramids at Giza on our fourth day in Egypt and had been granted entrance to the third largest pyramid. Never in my dreams had I imagined this would happen!

Rishi and I made our way down a small passageway of this colossal structure, down to an antechamber, then onwards to the burial chamber. It so happened that when we arrived inside this chamber we discovered that no-one else was there. We were completely alone within the pyramid of

Menkaure. The only way I can describe what I felt during the next ten minutes was 'a powerful sense of wellbeing'.

I sat down, cross-legged, closed my eyes and began to hum. My voice resonated so easily around the chamber that I couldn't help imagining that I was one of the high priests who oversaw the last burial rights of the great Pharaoh's remains. I felt as if I were being pulled back in time. After a few minutes I became aware that I'd better stop humming to not drive Rishi crazy! So I contented myself with sitting there with my back against the wall, taking it all in. I imagined the final hours of the burial ceremony: a great chorus of ancient Egyptian songs, chants and burial rituals. I tried to imagine the great glistening golden treasure being carried in and stored for the afterlife of the Pharaoh. As I sat there imagining all of this, a great feeling of happiness overcame me. This boy from Glenroy and Essendon was interacting with the souls of a different people who had lived 4,500 years ago!

Then I felt something else. I didn't see a ghostly apparition or hear any spectral voice, but I seemed to sense a presence of some kind. I opened my eyes, looked at Rishi and said quietly, "There's something or someone down here with us."

"It's probably your imagination, Dave," Rishi retorted.

I shrugged. I couldn't blame him for being sceptical. Much as I wanted to see what I was feeling, it was just an impression and most likely a fantasy.

As I pondered this, it dawned on me that my wish to see ancient Egypt as it used to be was never going to happen. The ancients weren't coming back. The white marble casing of the Pyramids wasn't going to magically re-appear on the worn down outer-stone structure. The beautiful temples weren't going to magically regain their colourful painted walls. I felt sad and a little helpless that I couldn't experience these great monuments and these ancient people in all their glory.

And then another thought struck me: *Nor could I go back to my kindergarten years.* My life was in the here-and-now. Why keep contemplating what it would be like to go back? The present was happening right now and the future was waiting for me. Sure, it was wonderful interacting with monuments of the past and imagining experiences of ancient times, but I couldn't bring old glories into the present in my personal life any more than the ancient Egyptians could wake up and start living among us again. It was time to move on – and take my past experiences with me.

In addition to America and Egypt, I experienced more of my country, Australia, every year with trips to places like Uluru (Ayers Rock) and Port Douglas. My father discounted travel, saying that it was nothing but a waste of money and it was wiser to invest. He had been encouraging me to buy property, either to invest in or to live in, and I have taken his advice in recent years as well, but the travel bug had me first and I am so grateful that it bit me and sent me on those adventures.

As for bringing the past to life, a few years later social media would offer me a portal through which I could find and reconnect with more past friends, and put to rest some old demons. In the meantime, a school reunion became the perfect opportunity for this.

OLD DISEMPOWERING RULE #9: Give up on my dreams. Don't believe anything special will happen to me. Live a small life.

NEW EMPOWERING RULE #10: Activate the power of my dreams. Take action on them. I deserve it.

Follow through on the courage of my convictions. Remember the days I struggled the most and hold true to the idea that one day I *will* achieve my dreams. It will be worth hanging in there. Back myself! Make a firm commitment. Invest in myself over time. If I'm handed lemons, make lemonade!

OLD DISEMPOWERING RULE #10: Hold onto illusions. Keep the past alive. Fantasise about how things could be 'if only'.

NEW EMPOWERING RULE #11: Let go of illusions. Leave the past in the past. Take realistic actions to realise my important dreams.

Understand that you only live once! Your time is a limited commodity and spending it by living or hiding in the past will block many possible positive experiences.

"There are years that ask questions, and years that answer."

– ZORA NEALE HURSTON

"Stop looking for happiness in the same place you lost it."

– ANONYMOUS

CHAPTER 10: An Old 'Feel Better By Eating' Rule is Transformed

"Gluttony is an emotional escape, a sign that something is eating us."

– PETER DE VRIES

In the aftermath of school I buried some of my frustration in poor habits. I seemed to have created the rule, 'Feel Better By Eating', and by 2002 my weight was getting out of control.

I had left school at 18 weighing around 85 kilograms. By 2002 my weight was up to 103 kg! I was coming home at night tired from hefting around all that extra weight, and still feeling tired in the morning after very little sleep because during the night I was consumed by endless depressing 'memory loops' of my challenging past.

All this would have continued if it hadn't been for one night when I went into Mum's room to say goodnight and she made a comment that stopped me in my tracks. She was in bed, and as I landed my backside on the edge of her bed it sagged quite a lot.

"Dave," she said, "I'm starting to worry about you."

"Why's that, Mum? What's wrong?"

"You're a lovely-looking boy but I fear you are letting yourself go."

I just stopped. Didn't say anything else. No-one had ever told me I was fat – or even too heavy.

"I think you should try and make some adjustments in your life, David," Mum continued. "I know your goals are important to you but it's going to become harder and harder to pursue them if you let yourself go much longer."

Now, when it's your own mum indicating that you're overweight and maybe even becoming obese, your whole perspective is suddenly changed. I realised, with a shock, that my excess weight was possibly costing me relationships with women.

I drove home in a daze after that discussion. I remember staggering through the door of my single-bedroom flat, slumping onto my couch and thinking, 'Crap! I thought something was working against me! Didn't realise how badly until now!'

Amazingly, the previous weekend I'd purchased the Tony Robbins classic, *Awaken the Giant Within*. That very night I opened it and got straight to work.

I say 'work', because that book requires work! You don't just read it; you have to do stuff along the way. It only took me one week to read because I was riveted; then I went back through and did all the exercises. *Awaken the Giant Within* sure woke me up. It shook me up! I realised that even since leaving school, my life had been governed by the rules I'd established from that era.

At the halfway mark into that book, I gritted my teeth and set about rewriting more of the rules that were governing my life. No more knockbacks from women for dates! No more struggling for breath as I tried to get up the third flight of stairs to my pokey little single-bedroom unit!

Anthony Robbins's ultimate chapter challenged me to answer fourteen questions that were spread across thirteen pages. His questions made me assume accountability for my actions. They helped me to look deep within myself and ask what I really wanted in my life and how I was going to get it. Over the course of one night, I wrote answers to every one of his questions. This time my life was going to be different!

Within four days I had joined a gym. My starting weight was 100 kilograms – I think I dropped a few kilos just in the process of shock from reading the book! The fitness instructor spelled out where I was and where I needed to be. I was handed a membership card. My goal was to take 100 grams off per visit.

I attended every class he signed me up for. I went to the gym religiously four times a week. I never tired of going. And my weight began to drop. My double chin grew thinner. I began to feel lighter and fitter.

Around the beginning of 2003 I received a call from a student I hadn't seen since leaving school. He told me that the 10-year reunion was being held in November that year. I felt a shiver down my spine and said I'd consider it.

Everybody I spoke to who knew me from school days suggested that I not go. My parents tried to dissuade me and several of my friends who knew about my troubled experiences were of that same opinion. I was on the verge of following their advice until I spoke to Grandad, Mum's dad.

We were still in recovery from the loss of his wife a few months before. He was my last grandparent and I felt a particular responsibility to absorb as much of his advice as I could, and to apply his wisdom. My grandad had served in the Second World War and, having watched and re-watched all the old World War II movies in my library many times, I had developed a particular interest in his generation. To me, he and his peers were special because they had been through such dire situations. He had attended reunions for his platoon for a few years after the ending of hostilities, so perhaps he would understand why I was drawn to go. He did.

"Son, I reckon it'll do you the world of good," he said. "You need some closure on that era and this may be your only opportunity to do it."

When Grandad spoke in that tone, I listened.

Later that night, I took a long walk around my old school. It was 12 a.m. and I still remember the pencil pines howling in each strong gust of wind. I leaned against the cyclone fence of my secondary school, listened to the wind, and stared at the main oval. An apparition took form in front of me. It was my first crush, Jo, appearing as the 12-year-old I remembered so well. I still missed her after all these years – even now as a 27-year-old. I'd learned that there was a good chance she was coming to the reunion and, as I'd discovered that she was engaged, I wanted one last chance to see her. I didn't want to become a stalker, even though I still craved contact. I wanted Jo to have a happy marriage without me hanging about so, as Grandad had advised, seeing her again would provide some closure.

November came quickly. I'd been training hard. My final weight on the night of the reunion was 78 kilograms! I'd lost 25 kilograms since Mum hinted that I had a problem.

The weight issue was important to me. My intention was to look completely transformed. I wanted my fellow students to see that 10 years away from school had changed me: I was now an experienced international sportsman in clay target shooting; I had travelled overseas and come face to face with the mummies of ancient Egypt and seen many other iconic structures; I had befriended people from distant lands; I had contributed greatly to the Presentation Awards industry, where thousands of articles I'd created had been received all around the land. I saw this night as my chance to come back to school and prove that I was successful and prospering.

I bought a suit for the night. I'd grown a small moustache to look a little more distinguished. Before leaving I had a few minutes to sit down and mentally prepare for the night. Were the kids who'd bullied me going to give me trouble, even though they were now adults? Was I to see my old teachers again? How was I going to react if I saw Jo? Would I have the guts to at least say hello to her? And what about the other girls in general? I'd found it hard to strike up conversations in Years 11 and 12 with the female students, who seemed to be dating all the other guys. It had appeared that the really good-looking ones were only interested in boys who played the major sports such as football, cricket and soccer. It didn't seem to matter that by this stage I wasn't a bad clay target shooter and was probably the only one in my year. The school didn't have an opening for target shooters and the girls weren't interested.

I psyched myself up for the reunion by playing the opening scene to *The Hunt for Red October*. Although I love the entire movie, the opening scene really resonates with me. It depicts a grey-haired Sean Connery gazing over the icy barren shores of Murmansk in his role as Captain Ramius. Captain Borodin, his first officer, comments in Russian, "It's cold today, Captain." Ramius answers almost dreamily, "Cold… and hard." It seems that Ramius has been stuck there in the Soviet Naval service for most of his life – a kind of prison sentence. Borodin looks at his captain and announces, "It's time, Captain." The Captain turns and says, "It's time… time indeed." The scene closes with the two men standing on the sail of Red October while the submarine is escorted out of the harbour by naval pilot ships.

It was easy, in my mind, to connect this scene to my school life. I was sailing out of my old harbour for the last time. It was time to find a new world by letting go of the past. I was hoping that my old school peers were no longer the immature teenagers I'd left behind and would be capable of a conversation with me about those troubled times. I was hoping to let go of the last of my supressed feelings for certain people, whether by having a civil conversation with them or by relating stories from those days at school and how they had affected me.

The Hunt for Red October was to be my anchor for the night. As you'll recall in Chapter 3, I had developed a system of creating 'anchors' or deliberate associations to positive states, and *Red October* was to be my inspiration that night. Although by this time I had changed my physical appearance, travelled and worked in my family business for ten years, competed in an international sport, and experienced the majestic monuments man has created in Egypt and in the United States, I had not been completely relieved of the torments of the past or the crazy desire to have a second chance at childhood. I needed closure and I needed to convince my spirit that there was no way I could turn the clock back.

I switched the TV off and caught a cab into town. I will admit that as I approached the entrance to the bar where the reunion was being held, a few sharp pangs of anxiety drowned out my *Red October* music and changed it to the scene in *Die Hard* when John McClane (played by Bruce Willis) finds himself trapped on top of the Nakatomi Plaza building where his only means of escape is to tie a fire hose around his waist and jump off the floor before the roof is blown up by terrorists. In that moment, his panicked voice keeps asking what he is doing and "How the hell did you get into this shit!"

When I walked into the pub that night the faces were all instantly recognisable. Memories came flooding back. But everyone had changed in demeanour. During the course of the first hour I came to realise that time had settled these young adults down. The reality of no longer being sheltered by their families and school had matured many of them – to say nothing of new lives with all-consuming careers and family responsibilities. And I was a completely different guy.

I enjoyed the first hour of great conversations with more humanised students than I had remembered. It turned out that while not so many of them remembered my chess or History results, some did remember those plaster and concrete projects I'd built with Dad, and most remembered me flying radio-controlled aircraft and teaching them how to operate the devices. (So I *had* made some sort of impact!)

After talking to a few people I made my way to the bar for another drink. I still remember standing there and surveying the room while I waited to be served. And suddenly she was there! Jo walked right up next to me, glancing at me as she passed.

"JO!" I grabbed her by both arms and looked her right in the eyes.

"Hey, Dave! You remember me?"

"How can I forget you?"

So now, because I had confronted my fears, I was able to finally meet up with my old crush.

There seemed so little time. We took a few photos, spoke of the times we had played together in the park, and I caught up on some of what had happened in her life after she left our school for another in 1990. Before I could summon the courage to speak with her about a fateful day in 1987, she had to excuse herself.

So I waited. I spoke to more ex-students but avoided the ones who had given me the most trouble. Some of those students hadn't shown up, including, to my relief, 'Biff'. Not that I would have gone out of my way to speak to him. I hadn't forgiven him for all the hardships I'd experienced and I still resented him for how he seemed to have gotten away with what he had done. I just wanted my night to run smoothly. Then, as the event was about to wind up, I managed to wangle a quiet word with Jo. I had been carrying this personal demon for 17 years and it was time. It just had to be done.

Jo was talking to one of her old friends. I discovered that she was about to marry someone whose surname sounded like the name of the boy she had gone out with in 1987. That triggered me...

As she turned toward me, I blurted, "Jo, I have to tell you something. I hope you'll be okay with this."

"What is it?" Jo gazed at me with the same sparkling look in her eyes she had as a child.

"I must tell you about a day that was pretty terrible for me."

"What happened?"

"It was a Friday. I had looked everywhere for you. I wanted to ask you out but couldn't conjure up the courage – I needed to talk to you privately but you were always surrounded by people. I thought I might have a chance in the locker area. But when I got there you were talking to that Tom fellow." I paused… then leapt in. "This is what I have to tell you, Jo: when we were at school I… I had a big crush on you."

Jo's jaw dropped. "Wow! I'm sorry, I didn't know, Dave!"

I hoped she wasn't offended by my confession but there was nothing I could do about it; I just wanted her to know how I'd felt. But I couldn't get another word out of her. She just got up and walked away to another side of the room. I felt surprised but I guessed that I had shocked her and perhaps she was worried about what to say next.

Nonetheless, my painful memories of Jo had been silenced and I actually felt elated! My 12-year-old self finally felt heard, he had been raised from the dead just long enough to be heard. A burden I'd carried around for 17 years had been lifted off my shoulders. The burden was my regret that I had never acted on my feelings for this girl. Those feelings of regret had haunted me for so long.

Back in 1987 I had made a pact with myself that on 'Jump Rope for Heart' Day I was going to ask Jo to go out with me. The girls and boys at my school had different campuses but for this event both groups came together, and as she was in my year, I had every reason to believe that Jo would turn up at my school. Since the event was to last for most of the day I reasoned that I could find Jo on her own and 'catch up with her' without being seen by the other boys or girls in my year. I did pass her a few times during the day, but she wasn't alone. So I waited. I tried to keep within sight of her without stalking her. It was exhausting.

After lunch, I decided to 'go on patrol' and see if I could find her. Surely there would be one moment I could spend with her without being noticed by anyone else! I walked around the ovals of the school but couldn't find her. She seemed to have disappeared. I headed toward our locker area and as I approached the corridor, I couldn't believe my luck. There she was!

'Okay, I'm going in!' I thought to myself.

All I could see was her silhouette in the light of the corridor. As I proceeded, bucking up the little courage I had, I noticed she was talking to someone. That someone was concealed by a rack of school bags. I hoped the person was one of her girlfriends.

But when I was within a few metres, I realised that she was being 'chatted up' by another student, a bully I had been having trouble with all year. Even at the age of 43, I can distinctly remember feeling my heart sinking at the sight of them together. *'Abort! Abort! Abort!'* I panicked. This wasn't the way it was supposed to go!

I walked on past them, trying not to reveal my shock. I was too late! My insecurity had got the better of me. I was too late! I should have acted earlier on my feelings for Jo. Now that opportunity was gone.

I walked out of the locker room, defeated. Of all the disappointments I'd met with in life, of all the bullying, of all my failures to this point in my life, I had never felt more gutted! I'd lost my chance of winning over the person I cared about more than anyone else!

Later in the afternoon, I saw her walking around the oval with this boy. He'd won! He had beaten me without even knowing it! Jo seemed so happy. All I could do was watch from a distance, trying to conceal my sorrow for fear of being mocked for it. It seemed like the beginning of spring for this newly formed couple; it was the end for me.

My problem here was that at the age of 12 I had created a limiting belief that I wouldn't be able to have a happy future unless I could be with one of the two girls I'd had a crush on since my kindergarten year. I understand that this seems like a very strange, even stupid belief, but my happiness was connected to the times of my early childhood. In my mind, with my parents' behaviour changing since the time of the factory inspector and with the ongoing bullying at school, I had been trying to hold onto elements of my childhood that had become 'personal sacred relics' of happiness.

The memory of that other boy's triumph that day had been a blunt, dull weapon slamming into my heart. With the hope of having Jo as my girlfriend gone, I had seemed doomed to isolation. I cannot ever remember feeling so lost and helpless. But now it didn't matter if we were never to see each other again; Jo would know that she was special to me.

Jo and I made contact once more at the end of the night. I shook hands with her fiancé and wished them both well for their wedding preparations. I was sad, a little jealous, but relieved at the same time.

When I got home I spoke to my 12-year-old self. This was the first time that I fully appreciated my choices and decisions that day with the gun. The 28-year-old version of me staring back in the mirror of my bedroom had my 12-year-old self to thank. It was due to the courage of that 12-year-old that I was still here to experience all that I had experienced to that moment. I felt very emotional. I thanked that 12-year-old for all the courage he had displayed and the burden he had carried.

It turns out that I *had* matured. I had made a contribution to the world by not attacking 'Biff'. I had achieved some goals I was proud of and I had faced some fears. Most importantly, I had discovered the value of conscious and consistent personal and physical development.

OLD DISEMPOWERING RULE #11: Feel better by eating. Soothe my anxiety and depression by unhealthy lifestyle habits such as poor diet and alcohol.

OLD DISEMPOWERING RULE #12: Suffer and feel the pain of regret.

NEW EMPOWERING RULE #12: Be humble about receiving honest feedback from those who love me. (E.g. Mum)

NEW EMPOWERING RULE #13: Flip the coin! Make fitness and proper diet a priority to give me the leverage to build up my self-esteem and confidence. (The benefits to me far outweigh the pain of self-discipline.)

NEW EMPOWERING RULE #14: Honour and respect my body by eating well and exercising regularly. (The benefits to me far outweigh the pain of self-discipline.)

NEW EMPOWERING RULE #15: Do the self-development work (E.g. Anthony Robbins' questions) **because the insights I gain will motivate me to create long-lasting change.**

NEW EMPOWERING RULE #16: Face old fears and do the things I need to do to achieve closure on old, troubling experiences.

I have nothing to lose by expressing caring to another person. If my actions don't have the desired effect, at least I can walk away knowing that I behaved nobly. (I discovered that the benefits to me far outweighed the anxiety I felt at the thought of attending that reunion and telling Jo how I felt.)

NEW EMPOWERING RULE #17: No matter how long it takes or what it takes, hang on to my important dreams and live them. (If I hang on, I will realise that dream one way or another!)

NEW EMPOWERING RULE #18: Instead of allowing myself to be imprisoned by past experiences, keep my mind open to new possibilities.

To this day I instruct my clients and dance students to always back themselves and invest in themselves. The money and time they trade to increase their knowledge will open new doors for them. But it isn't just about them; it's also about what they can do for their fellow man or woman, or even a fellow creature. How can they improve the quality of life of another person or creature? How will they apply and share their knowledge? The possibilities are endless!

What are the new rules *you* have created for yourself as a result of reading this chapter? Add them to your notebook.

"Don't be scared to try and fail; be afraid to fail to try."

– EDMOND MBIAKA

"I have the courage to live out my dreams."

– LOUISE HAY

Summary Of My Old And New Rules To Date

Old Disempowering Rules

    Chapter 3

OLD RULE #1: Follow the rules at home and at school. Conform. Do what I'm told. Try to fit in.

OLD RULE #2: Believe I'm unworthy. Put my power outside of myself, in other people. Live at the effect of their opinion of me. Take their taunts personally. Believe their judgemental views of me are right and are the whole truth about me. Be suspicious and nervous of every little facial expression and movement others make, taking them all personally as being about me.

OLD RULE #3: Be resentful of anything that isn't going my way. Believe that life isn't fair.

OLD RULE #4: Expect others to dominate me. Expect to be bullied. Respond by playing victim.

OLD RULE #5: Decide that it's all too hard. Stop trying. Get upset when people tell me to lift my game.

    Chapter 5

OLD RULE #6: Listen to (and believe) destructive self-talk. Listen to and believe the critical comments of others.

    Chapter 6

OLD RULE #7: Fight to survive!

    Chapter 7

OLD RULE #8: React! Avenge myself! Block the little voice of my conscience! Get even! Pay back!

Chapter 9

OLD RULE #9: Give up on your dreams. Don't believe anything special will happen to me. Live a small life.

OLD RULE #10: Hold onto illusions. Keep the past alive. Fantasise about how things could be 'if only'.

Chapter 10

OLD RULE #11: Feel better by eating. Soothe my anxiety and depression by unhealthy lifestyle habits such as poor diet and alcohol.

OLD RULE #12: Suffer and feel the pain of regret.

New Empowering Rules

Chapter 4

NEW RULE #1: Instead of meekly going along with everything look for ways to express myself, stand out, and be a nonconformist!

NEW RULE #2: Find my past friends, those who share a happier history with me, and choose new friends who share similar values.

NEW RULE #3: *The original version was:* **'Don't spread ugly rumours about other students. Do everything I can to avoid a fight, but if unfairly picked on for one and I can't win on the day, wait six months and then get back at them – on my terms!'**

The more mature David Gillman changed this to: **'Train in self-defence in a secure environment. Seek to build rapport wherever possible with my fellow students. Don't waste any energy trying to appease those who simply wish to use me for their amusement. They're not worth worrying about!'**

NEW RULE #4: Reach out to an older generation – people I can trust, people I can confide in, maybe someone who has strategies I can use to keep me safe and sane.

NEW RULE #5: Find out what really excites me in life!

NEW RULE #6: Instead of listening to people who don't understand me and frustrate me, learn from the history books!

Chapter 5
NEW RULE #7: Consciously choose which voice I listen to. Listen to the Most Empowering Voice, whether internal or external.

Chapter 6
NEW RULE #8: Avoid fighting wherever possible but if there is no escaping a fight, a strong beginning can bring it to an end much sooner than my opponent expects, so be in the strongest mental and physical condition I can. If I think I am likely to be picked on frequently, consider enrolling in self-defence classes.

Chapter 7
NEW RULE #9: Think twice before acting in vengeance. Choosing to not harm others is much more empowering than choosing to lash out; self-control is a far more impressive ability than reactivity. When contemplating revenge on anyone, interrupt that pattern by sitting quietly and allowing my mind to coach me to a solution.

Chapter 9
NEW RULE #10: Activate the power of my dreams. Act on them. I deserve it.

NEW RULE #11: Let go of illusions. Leave the past in the past. Take realistic actions to realise my important dreams.

Chapter 10
NEW RULE #12: Be humble about receiving honest feedback from those who love me. (E.g. Mum)

NEW RULE #13: Flip the coin! Make fitness and proper diet a priority to give me the leverage to build up my self-esteem and confidence. (The benefits to me far outweigh the pain of self-discipline.)

NEW RULE #14: Honour and respect my body by eating well and exercising regularly. (The benefits to me far outweigh the pain of self-discipline.)

NEW RULE #15: Do the self-development work (E.g. Anthony Robbins' questions) **because the insights I gain will motivate me to create long-lasting change.**

NEW RULE #16: Face old fears and do the things I need to do to achieve closure on old, troubling experiences.

NEW RULE #17: No matter how long it takes or what it takes, hang on to my important dreams and live them. (If I hang on, I will realise that dream one way or another!)

NEW RULE #18: Instead of allowing myself to be imprisoned by past experiences, keep my mind open to new possibilities.

Chapter 11: OLD RULE: Stay In Your Comfort Zone

NEW RULE: Take A Risk! Get out there and invest in yourself.

"If you can't get rid of the skeleton in the closet you'd best take it out and teach it to dance."

– GEORGE BERNARD SHAW

I find myself walking the streets of my home suburb, Essendon. The sky is overcast. It is winter and the leaves in the trees are all shrivelled and falling. The streets are cold and nearly empty. There are prominent cracks in the asphalt. I notice old people hobbling along the road. There's no breeze, no birds singing, just a sense of foreboding. I feel desolate, numb.

I somehow make it home. My family home feels more like a lifeless run-down house than a home. It is dusty and dank. Much of the furniture is gone. No evidence of happiness from the previous decades remains. There is nothing but the prospect of an empty lonely existence into the future. My adulthood is nothing like I imagined it as a child...

For many years after leaving school I woke up from this dream. My original school friends were running about town working, dating or getting married but I was still single, lonely, disappointed with myself, and feeling that my life was mediocre. Even though I'd lost the weight and had achieved the things I'd achieved, I still felt inadequate by comparison with others.

A few weeks after the school reunion, I lay on my back in my single-bedroom unit and stared up at the ceiling, contemplating my life. I literally had so much on my mind I couldn't move. I began to ask myself some questions...

Who Am I?

What am I doing here?

Am I happy and don't know it?
What are the results of my existence over the last 28 years?
Was it worth holding onto my life?
Were all my effort to improve my fitness worth it?
Why am I still alone?
What is yet to come?
What difference have I made to my family and friends?
What difference have I made in this world?
Should I be proud of what I have accomplished so far or is it still not good enough?
Where do I go from here?

The upshot of all those questions was that I was still lonely. The 10-year school reunion had helped awaken in me the realisation that it was time to move on from my childhood thoughts, fears and desires. Many of my peers were engaged, married or already had children. I still had none of that. It was beginning to really concern me that I had not yet found someone to love, someone who would love me…

I had sold my unit and used the equity to purchase some acreage on the border of Sunbury, a semi-rural suburb of Melbourne. In order to afford this property I'd had to move back in with my parents. Urghh! That wasn't good. I really wanted my own house now! But first I had to save money to pay off the land so that I could build my house and be ready for my future wife.

I began to work even harder in the family business. When I couldn't work long hours or didn't feel like going to the gym I walked the family dog. Each long walk during that long year of 2003 and into 2004 reminded me of how lonely I was.

One day in February 2004 I passed a dance studio on my way home. It was nearly 10 p.m. and it sounded like they were having a ball up there on the second floor. I stopped and contemplated the source of music and laughter for a few minutes. I looked at the dog, looked up at a window of the studio, then looked down at the dog again. "Chester, you're staying home tomorrow night."

Now at that stage of my life dancing was the very last thing I wanted to do! I was a shooter and wanted to meet my future wife shooting or performing in some masculine sport. Ballroom dancing seemed way down the opposite end of the spectrum. But I wasn't doing very well in my love life, and I was haunted by the memory of the Debutante Ball at school in Year 12.

Ninety per cent of our year attended that Debutante Ball but I spent the night moping in my room. I'd asked one girl to go to the Deb with me, but her excuse was so pathetic that I'd assumed *no-one* wanted to go with me. And it seemed I was right: much as I'd hoped someone would ask me, no-one did. I figured I was being avoided because I wasn't popular so I didn't try asking anyone else.

I spent the night of the Deb Ball stuck at home, playing on my computer in my dark bedroom, imagining most of my friends and the other school students of my year having a great time dressing up, being driven by limo to the event hall, and having a wonderful night dancing. This was one of the lowest periods of my teenage years. It had me drifting into deep depression and even starting to contemplate suicide again. For years afterwards I would revisit the events of this night over and over again in my mind, alone and lonely.

But the core of pain for this incident was located much earlier in my history – back in those kindergarten days when I fell in love with a beautiful young girl with sausage curls. When I say 'fell in love', I mean that I did everything I could to be with her. I pursued her as effectively as a four-year-old boy could do, but Heidi just wanted to hang out with the other girls. I used to come home full of happiness, wondering if there was any chance that she'd come over and play with me and my toys in my backyard. I wanted to play her my favourite vinyl records. I wanted to introduce her to my entire family.

One day my feelings for her became so overpowering that I proudly announced to Mum that I was going to marry Heidi. I still remember my mother laughing at me. And I remember feeling a wave of guilt or shame, although I didn't understand why. The next time we went to visit my grandparents Mum said, "David, tell Grandma what you told me a few days ago about someone you like?"

I looked at my grandmother squarely in the eyes and proudly announced that I was going to marry Heidi. Both ladies cackled with laughter, and while I didn't understand the concept of mockery, I felt mocked. It was as if my mother had walked into my newly discovered and favourite pastime, and sullied my enjoyment.

I carried that embarrassment with me from that day as a four-year-old. It became difficult to interact with Heidi the next day at kindergarten, and it affected my other relationships too. Since I was a single child and my parents worked such long hours, I was often alone and didn't have much experience developing resilience in the face of teasing. When I developed my crush on Jo, my past experience of sharing delicate feelings with my then closest confidante and mentor (Mum) and being laughed at resulted in a decision to keep my romantic affections hidden. The effect on my confidence was significant.

Now, 24 years after my Heidi crisis and 11 years after being rejected at the School Deb, I was going to make sure that I didn't miss out again. It was time to turn another governing belief on its head. It was time to rewrite the Disempowering Rule: *'Feel Mocked'* and create a new Empowering Rule that said: *'Keep Trying. Believe in yourself. Trust that you are worthy. Have a go.'*

I tried three times to get through the doors of the Essendon Danse Academy (Yes, that is the actual spelling). The first night I tried to enter they were playing some really sooky, lovey-dovey sounding music. I had my hand on the door but couldn't push through.

I tried again about four nights later. I had been walking the dog and brooding about how trapped I felt. It was now or never. Somehow I conjured up the courage to once again leave the dog at home and walk through that door and up the stairs.

The music wasn't so bad that night. I took a deep breath at the top of the stairs… and walked into the dance studio. There were around eight couples of different ages from 18 years to 70+ in a circle, dancing away. A very distinguished, well-postured middle-aged lady noticed me standing at the front desk and gracefully walked over to me, asking, "What may I do for you?"

"I'm wondering if I could join up for lessons," I replied nervously.

"You'll have to come back tomorrow, hun. Beginner Classes start at 7:30."

"I have no partner. Will that be okay?"

"You'll be fine, hun. Most of you guys start without one. We'll look after you."

I walked out. Damn! I had been ready to bite the bullet and start that night. Urghh! I'd conjured up the guts to walk through that door only to be stalled. 'Oh well,' I thought, 'it begins tomorrow.'

That first lesson – phew! I was nervous! Not only did I have a preconception of dancing as not very masculine, but I also had a debilitating memory of three girls who cut me out of a progressive dance at school back in Year 11 or 12. I'd been enjoying these classes, especially because I could be in close contact with many of the girls I found attractive, but one day it all fell apart.

I noticed three girls looking at me and whispering, and optimistically hoped that they were interested in me – especially the one I was interested in! But when I met up with the first of these girls in the progressive circle dance she was very cold and aloof. I didn't pay too much attention, but when it was time for me to partner up with the girl I was interested in, she flung her hands up in the air and went straight to the boy next to me. I tried to act cool and dance on my own, but when I came face-to-face with the third girl, she did the same thing! I tried to break in but was shoved out. Disillusioned, I slunk to the side of the floor and stopped dancing. In fact, I abandoned that class for the rest of the term. My pride was so injured that for many years after I was hypersensitive to rejection by any woman, whether on the dance floor or in relationship.

So between painful past memories and the challenge of learning a new skill from scratch I was very awkward during that first class. Fortunately I realised that I had to leave my ego at the door – it was costing me too much to stay in the past. So I did manage to push those troubling memories away. I sensed the potential of this new activity both as a form of exercise and as a way of meeting women, and I hung in there.

My initial plan was to simply learn basic dance steps, go to a bar or club, pick up the future Mrs Gillman, and live happily ever after. If you were to have told me what was to follow after three months of dance classes I would have scoffed at you and said, "Nah, not me! I'm a shooter!"

But three months after that first lesson the owner of the studio, Richard, invited me to prepare for a medal exam. I didn't think I was ready to dance a medal but he assured me that I was more than capable. Now, dance sport is an institution that is plagued by a shortage of men. In the competition arena there are often ten girls to one boy, so dance studios are always very interested when a new man signs up for classes, especially one who is determined to do well. And I was determined! I trained and trained and trained. I even repeated the beginner class. I looked admiringly at the more advanced medal dancers and marvelled when some of the top dancers of the school demonstrated for us. They just seemed so out of this world in confidence.

I was invited to observe the mid-year exams at the studio where I discovered, to my relief, that students were presented to the examiner by the teacher rather than dancing with other students. Richard and the other teachers made their students look good!

I went home that night thinking about the exams I'd observed. I still remember waking up from a nightmare the next morning: I was standing on the edge of the dance floor. An adjudicator sat at a table and Richard's partner Sam, who was my designated dance partner, was staring at me as if totally perplexed and annoyed that I hadn't prepared for the exam. My name was announced, the blank exam paper was presented to me to give to the examiner for his assessment, and I was in a cold sweat!

That nightmare frightened me into making the commitment to be prepared! If I was going to dance with Sam, Dave Gillman, the veteran clay target shooter, wasn't going to let her down.

It was seven months before I danced my Bronze Medal. This exam is the lowest level in the medal system: it's where the student demonstrates the basics. I was so determined to do well that I'd gone beyond the Bronze Medal Beginner Class – I'd taken private lessons. I'd practised and practised and practised. I wasn't going to let my teacher down and I wasn't going to let myself down.

On the day of the Medal my parents and Grandad came to observe. All my classmates were watching. I still remember taking Sam's hand proudly and walking up to the adjudicator. I was very nervous. But four dances later I was marked with Honours for each dance!

A few more years passed. More dance medals. I never dropped below Honours. I was still driven by the haunting memory of being rejected, first by Heidi and then by the girls at the school Deb, and now I was determined to be seen by my peers as an up-and-coming talent.

I started attending social dances run by other dance schools and began to mix with women of different ages and abilities. I was interacting with different people now, people who respected me as a dancer. The rule of self-investment was beginning to pay dividends in mental and physical fitness. In fact, all the lifestyle changes I'd made were beginning to have an effect on my personality. My personal confidence rose and I was no longer displaying signs of self-deprecation. I walked straighter and taller, my belief in myself was beginning to flourish, and I was making more friends. Soon I began dating.

By the beginning of 2006, the new rules that determined who I associated with, how I thought about my past, and how I used its negative effects for positive purposes in my life had taken root. No longer would I be controlled by emptiness of the spirit and disappointment! I was re-writing the rules of my life for my benefit. The following dream was the last one I had in which I was wandering around the streets of my home suburb:

The entire scene is grey. No colour. Just bleakness. Instead of walking home to escape this desolation for the usual desolation, I turn a different corner. I know of a church there and I decide to approach it for the first time. I hesitate in front of the church. It stands out from the surrounding environment. It is a red brick and weatherboard dwelling. No-one seems to be outside but I venture to the door like a vagabond. I knock on a thick oak door. An elderly priest – white collar, black robe – answers.

"Sir," I tell him. "I need a place to stay. I am homeless and lonely. I am happy to do whatever it takes to help out here for a bed and a roof."

"Come, my boy," he replies. "We happen to have a spare hammock you can use."

I follow him to a side room at the back of the church. Another young man greets me in this room, helps me unload my few possessions and advises what time supper is.

"By the way," he adds, "practice for the Great Festival is on at six. Come and join us."

OLD RULE: STAY IN YOUR COMFORT ZONE. NEW RULE: TAKE A RISK!

I make my way to a great hall and survey the massive room, which is vibrating with a cacophony of people's voices and music. There are boys and girls, men and women of all ages dressed in magnificent if somewhat absurd costumes. Some are practising their lines for a play. Others are practising an interpretive dance they are to perform. The room is full of colour. Everyone is cheerful and excited about what is to come...

I woke up refreshed. I felt full of hope and positivity. I wondered, though, at the dream. It seemed significant. Most of my dreams seemed to remind me of people I'd lost along the way, or undesirable events that kept me from my ultimate goals in life but this one felt much more optimistic.

As I prepared to get up for work I reached for my mobile phone and noticed a message from Richard, my dance teacher. He was looking for a male competition dance partner for a young lady student of his and was wondering if I was interested.

This proved to be the beginning of a journey that resulted in me competing seriously for 14 years with a number of different partners, and winning several prestigious awards.

I would like to thank all those who had a hand in my rescue. That means every person I met from the moment I walked in that door at Essendon Danse Academy. To all those ladies, and their boyfriends or husbands who lent me their partners while I improved myself through dance practice, I pay homage. These women are probably as ignorant of their role in saving me as 'Biff' was of my decision to step back and let him go on to live a rich life, but perhaps they will one day read this book and understand the magic they helped to create in welcoming me, dancing with me and advising me/instructing me/giving me tips. As a token of my thanks for their kindness to me, I will always dance with any woman who asks me, even if she is a raw beginner.

I took up dancing as a means of finding a wife, but what I learned is that you cannot pursue this pastime thinking it's a dating service; it's far more than that. Sure, you will learn dance steps, but more importantly, you will become a contributor to others' wellbeing and to your own personal growth, because dancing has the potential to take you to new heights of awareness. And your physical fitness will boom.

That said, I did meet my beautiful wife Vivienne at a dance studio, and not only does she dance but she can also shoot! I met the future Mrs Gillman at another dance school, Star Studios, in 2006. At the time Vivienne turned me down for a dance because she had just broken up with her long-time boyfriend and was not yet ready to meet new men. Not knowing that, and still being affected by those three girls who saw to it that I was excluded from the progressive dance during Year 12, I'd assumed she was rejecting me because she didn't think I was a good enough dancer. The outcome was that I practised longer and harder, and when I saw her at the studio again a few years later in 2011, I was much more confident about approaching her, knowing that I was a far better dancer than when we had first met. One dance led to another, and very soon we were having weekend social trips out to wineries and restaurants. Had I have taken a resentful attitude to Viv and assumed she was just another arrogant girl we would never have become a romantic couple. My old belief system would have undermined me again!

OLD DISEMPOWERING RULE #13: Stay in your comfort zone.

NEW EMPOWERING RULE #19: Take a risk. Get out there and invest in yourself.

OLD DISEMPOWERING RULE #14: Feel mocked. Every time you are challenged, draw the boundaries of your world inward to where you feel safe and comfortable.

NEW EMPOWERING RULE #20: Keep Trying. Believe in yourself. Trust that you are worthy. Have a go. Take wise risks!

NEW EMPOWERING RULE #21: Seek knowledge and experience in new fields. These 'new worlds' will open up my mind and skills beyond what I might have imagined possible.

NEW EMPOWERING RULE #22: Express gratitude to those who play a pivotal role in my life.

"I used to care about what people thought about me, until one day, I tried to pay my bills with their opinions."

– ANONYMOUS

"Take pride in how far you have come and have faith in how far you can go."

– CHRISTIAN LARSON

'Make it happen! Shock everyone!'

– UNKNOWN, FOUND ON PINTEREST

CHAPTER 12: Important Friendships Are Worth Waiting For

"Let come what comes, let go what goes. See what remains."

– RAMANA MAHARSHI

I am a ghost, though I haven't realised it. I am floating around the main hall of what seems to be St. John's Uniting Church. All the students of my year, boys, girls and teachers of 1988, are attending a memorial service. They are all in school uniform. I am listening to the school reverend, Mrs Payne. When my name is mentioned at the beginning of the service, I grow angry. I realise I have followed through with my suicide.

In a fit of paranormal rage, I descend into the pews where the students are sitting. I see some of the students snickering at the service and others pretending they care. My spirit blasts through their chests and out through their backs! I let out a ghastly shriek causing the affected students to jump up out of their seats. Some of them run out of the church, terrified! I rise to an overhanging light and cause it to swing wildly above the heads of the students.

Then, as I pause to observe my effects over the hall, Mrs Payne calmly rests her Bible on the pulpit surface. She makes her way quietly to a girl who sits a few rows away from the front, a beautiful brunette who I identify as my childhood crush, Jo. Mrs Payne murmurs something into the ear of the young girl. Jo rises serenely and walks to the front of the hall, through to the private chamber, and closes the door. I follow her, passing through the wall. She stands there, not looking up or down or around, just gazing ahead. I instantly realise that the girl has been sent out of the hall so I may converse with her. I am moved by the gesture.

"I know it's you, David," she begins. "It was in the letter you left for us."

I am instantly disarmed. My ghostly apparition, nothing more than fog, *descends to her level. She turns, almost shyly, looking in the direction of my apparition, smiling with both eyes and lips as only she could. "I won't forget you..."*

With these disarming words, I forgive everyone in the church and ascend through the ceiling in peace...

I awoke but didn't move. My feelings about Jo were still unresolved. She was sacred to me: I still thought about how we would play together in the park over the road from where we both lived after our kindergarten year. I really missed her. She haunted me, and for decades I had been powerless to do anything about my feelings for her.

On many a lonely dark night during my 'singles' years, I would walk the family dog so far and for so long that we would make it to the old kindergarten. I would observe the faint orange streetlight glowing from a distance against the silhouetted building. I would imagine Jo there and in the park where we'd played, and hope that by some miracle she would appear on my nightly stroll. It never happened.

The Rule 'Hold Onto Your Dreams' whipped me like a cruel, taunting taskmaster. I would never be able to realise the dream of a closer relationship with Jo because she was now married. But as I had also moved on, I found myself remembering the indigenous wisdom that we don't own the Earth but are guardians of it; likewise, our lives present us with opportunities for growth rather than stuff or people to keep. Jo was not mine to 'have'; instead, my vision transformed from having her as my girlfriend or wife to having her as my friend.

The 20th school anniversary approached. I was invited and I took my fiancée Vivienne with me. For the first time, I was walking in there with physical proof that I had moved on, that I was loved, that I was successful in my own right.

It turned out that Jo decided to turn up again too! I was so happy to see her. This time I was absolutely no threat to her relationship with her husband. The night seemed to go smoothly and within a short time Jo and I had become Facebook friends along with two other women of the same era.

Shortly after, Vivienne and I planned a trip to Bendigo so Viv could sit her shooter's license. I figured that this would be a great opportunity for me to visit Jo and her husband since they lived in Bendigo. I figured that since Viv would be sitting her exam, I would finally have the time for a proper catch-up with Jo.

When I contacted Jo with this idea, I discovered that she and her husband had separated. I really thank Vivienne for trusting me to do the right thing by her. It's probably not normal for a fiancée to drop off her future husband at the home of another pretty woman, especially one she knows her fiancé was in love with for many years... But I was visiting with the intention of being heard. I wanted to resurrect my old friendship with Jo and this was the chance I'd been waiting for. In the car with me was my twelve-year-old self, eager to catch up with his childhood playmate.

Viv dropped me off at Jo's house and drove away. I was a little nervous but I was warmly welcomed and introduced to Jo's sons. We opened a bottle of red and sat down to dinner. After her children had gone to bed and over the course of the next few hours I shared everything that had happened. I told her about the day she appeared to walk off with one of the boys who was bullying me, the deep depression I had fallen into, my suicide attempt, walking the streets at night, and even seeing her apparition at the kindergarten. I laid it all out for her, and the result was the greatest weight off my shoulders that I'd ever experienced. Then Jo filled me in on her history, and it was jaw-dropping.

To begin with, everything between Jo and the boy she 'walked off into the sunset with' was fine. But three weeks later, when she went to greet him at the train station near school, 'Tom' refused to talk to her. He made a rude gesture at her and then walked away. A week after that she saw him sitting in a bus. She went to wave to him as the bus was pulling away... and he spat at her through the open window.

A little research into what was behind his obnoxious behaviour revealed that Tom had been using Jo to get to another girl at our school. That was all she needed to know to realise that this boy wasn't worth her energy. She had enough other problems on her plate, including the divorce of her parents.

This story was jaw-dropping for me not because of that boy's despicable behaviour, but because back when I was 12 their relationship was one of the reasons I had found myself sitting on my parents' couch cradling a gun in my lap. I had been convinced that I'd lost Jo to 'Tom'. As it turned out, a relationship between the two of them *hadn't even existed*, and my false belief that I would never have a chance to ask her out again had been entirely wrong. I could have had the girl of my dreams back then – and I'd have treated her a whole lot better than that guy!

After Jo finished relating this story, I apologised for not asking her out before he had.

"I wish you had," was Jo's reply.

It was a bittersweet moment, but that night, a great friendship was rekindled and a priceless lesson was learnt: *Don't assume anything. If it really matters to you, ask anyway.*

In a way, my dream of the church scenario at the start of this chapter was realised! Jo listened to my tormented soul, spoke of her own experience and feelings, and subsequently helped me to find peace.

Vivienne returned around 10:30 and we had a three-way conversation until one o'clock in the morning. It was one of the most surreal events I'd ever experienced.

To all of you who are haunted and unable to put to rest that which haunts you, I encourage you to either make contact with the other person directly (if possible and appropriate) and achieve the closure you are seeking, or to write a letter in which you express all your feelings and regrets and hopes – and then burn it. Even if the person has passed on, you will feel better. Your mind will be freed to pursue other goals, dreams and tasks. Some people may be able to self-heal quickly; others, like myself, need actual physical closure.

As the famous New Testament proverb goes:

Ask, and you shall receive.
Seek, and you shall find.
Knock, and the door shall be opened unto you.

For everyone who asks, receives.
And every seeker finds.
And to all those who knock, the door is open.

My dream of resolution with Jo was a long held intention; I was determined to leave this thread of my life dangling rather than cut it off. In the end it didn't matter how long it took to be realised.

What do *you* want to manifest? Meditate on this question and list your desires in your notebook. Then explore your options. If your desire involves someone else, ask yourself honestly if direct contact is appropriate. If not, is it better for you to make a symbolic connection with this person, either through writing a letter or visualising them and speaking to them?

List your desires and how you would like to manifest them.

"In the end, we only regret the chances we didn't take."

– LEWIS CARROLL

"Don't stress about the closed doors behind you. New doors are opening if you keep moving forward."

– THELMA DAVIS

"Maybe it's not about trying to fix something that's broken; maybe it's about starting over and creating something better."

– UNKNOWN

CHAPTER 13: Strategies For Success

"Keep some room in your heart for the unimaginable."

– MARY OLIVER

In the previous chapters, I've used my experiences to take us on a journey. I've explained that my life started very happily, then spiralled downward into a deep dark depression to a low point that saw me sitting on a couch with a decision to make: put an end to seemingly endless pain, or keep living in the hope that somehow my luck would turn and my life would begin to pick up again.

My initial plan for staying alive was quite rudimentary but it was my 'line in the sand'. No more retreating! No more giving up on my dreams of fulfilment! No more going to the back of the line when I wanted to participate! I was no longer prepared to have my personal development stunted because of others' rules. If I couldn't immediately turn a situation to my advantage, then I would work toward that outcome. I had every right to have a happy, fulfilling life. I would no longer let others stand in my way!

Over time I refined that basic plan and developed more skills, and the dreams that had seemed too good to be true were all fulfilled by the time I was in my 30s. I made friends, travelled, married, and stood out in a field of endeavour that mattered to me. None of that would have been possible without the guidance of friends, teachers, mentors, coaches and self-help books along the way.

I am one of many people who believe that school never really ends, particularly when it comes to your career and understanding the behaviour of the people around you. Zig Ziglar, the famous motivational speaker, said that over the course of a year, a driver stuck in traffic and using his car as an 'automobile university' can learn as much as a college student attending a year's worth of classes.

It is through all these resources that I was able to learn and apply strategies that have enabled me to transform my life. Those books and courses have turned out to be the best investments I've ever made. The skills and resources I've developed as a result have become invaluable assets. It's worthwhile repeating this quote:

> "Sometimes the bad things that happen in our lives put us directly on the path to the best things that will ever happen to us."
>
> – NICOLE REED

Before I list the strategies I found most useful in rebuilding my life, I would like to point out one thing: all the personal goals I've achieved were realised because I had a *hunger* to realise them. I didn't dabble; I was *driven* to reduce my pain and increase my sense of satisfaction with my life. This is the direct benefit of pain: if we have a too comfortable life we're probably not likely to have the drive and hunger to improve our circumstances.

The strategies that helped me to transform my life:

1. Notice what makes you come alive, what motivates you, what energises you – and do it!

Which activities and experiences make you happy? Actively pursue them. Develop those skills. Invest in yourself by using whatever resources you have! Instead of thinking you should be a better soccer player (like the others), be the best chess player you can be (since you actually like chess – or whatever!). The more you develop your genuine abilities and interests, the more you are building the life of your dreams, a life that will deliver a worthwhile return on time and energy invested.

For me, this meant following up on my interest in clay target shooting rather than trying to fit in with what everyone else was doing. It meant pursuing those kindergarten friendships when the people around me were not receptive. It meant watching old movies and studying history. *What does it mean for you?*

Investing in yourself is not selfish. Why? Because the only person who can truly help you when you're caught in the grips of a problem is you! You are the one in charge of your life! You need to make the critical decisions about who is to be in your life, what your career will be, what sport you will play, etc., and take risks that inspire YOU because this is YOUR life.

What makes *you* come alive? Make a comprehensive list in your notebook.

> "Ignoring your passion is a slow suicide. Never ignore what your heart pumps for. Mould your career around your lifestyle, not your lifestyle around your career."
>
> — INTELLIGENCE.COM

> "The cost of not following your heart is spending the rest of your life wishing you had."
>
> — SPIRIT SCIENCE

> "Sometimes life is about risking everything for a dream no-one can see but you."
>
> — ANONYMOUS

2. Create a big and exciting bucket list!

Most people are familiar with the idea of a bucket list: a list of life experiences we want to have before we die. Now it's time to create yours! Don't worry at this stage about *how* you're going to attain those things; just brainstorm wildly and fill your mind with possibility.

Answer the following questions in your notebook. Be as specific as you can.
1. What experiences would you love to have? How would you like your life to be and how would you like to feel? What do you hope for?
2. What type of friends are you seeking? What is their character? What are their interests?
3. What career would make you happy?
4. Is there a hobby you've always wanted to participate in, or a sport you've always wanted to play that you can now own up to?
5. Which powerful goal genuinely matters to you?

Experience all of this in your mind as you write it down. All physical, external success comes from the imagination, from an idea deep inside us. The imagination is so powerful and useful to us because it requires us to dream of new possibilities that will enable us to move towards a positive outcome, a new future. Our dreams and ambitions can generate magic.

You can stimulate the brainstorming process by looking through magazines or on the Internet for pictures that represent what you want to experience. Look around you at what is possible, and look within yourself.

If you want a hard copy of these images, create a 'vision board' by printing them out and arranging them on a sheet of poster paper or corkboard. If having your vision board easily visible to family and friends concerns you, store it in a hidden file on your computer. If you are looking for inspiration, I suggest viewing Pinterest, which is currently a very popular tool for creating vision boards.

We can create constructive images as easily as destructive images. Once you experience the positive power of your imagination you will find yourself facing in a whole new direction, one in which your life can be rich and fulfilling rather than sad and lonely. (NB. Steer your mind toward positive values only, and express those values in the positive. I.e. 'Friends' rather than 'Not lonely'. Also, make sure that no-one else will be harmed in the realisation of your dreams.)

Record your Bucket List and Goals. Be as specific as possible and list in your notebook.

3. Connect with your ideal values

Our values are our principles, our moral code of conduct, our standard of behaviour. When life is difficult for us it is often because we are focused on disempowering rules or values. However as we mature and grow, our values mature too. Now could be a good time for you to observe the values you are currently living by, and to consciously choose what is important to you.

Connecting with your ideal values is the best way to rewrite the rules of your life because those ideal values keep you focused on the best 'you' you can be. Mine included the following:

Happiness
Fulfilment
Love
Security
Purpose
Contribution
Creation
Enjoyment
Prosperity

Stating your values as single words stamps the meaning in your mind and heart instantly! That word may trigger a picture or a movie on the screen of your mind, or a physical sensation, or just simply a sense of meaning for you. Whatever our values, they are sacred to us.

How did I arrive at my ten values? Simply put, my spirit was starving for them! I felt emptiness, a void of happiness, fulfilment, love, etc., and so those qualities were of particular importance to me. Often what we perceive as most missing becomes the thing we most value and crave.

It's important that we ground those concepts in specific examples of how they would show up in our lives. This is what those words meant to me as a 12-year old:

1. Happiness: The energy and enthusiasm to go about my life. I am no longer bullied! I do great at school! My fellow students look to me for support. My teachers love working with me. My parents are no longer unhappy, anxious or depressed but are once again their old selves, working towards a more prosperous future.
2. Fulfilment: I have attained everything I wanted for my happiness. I no longer crave what my soul wants but feels it cannot have.
3. Love: I am surrounded by a loving family and loving friends. (I hoped that would include Jo!)
4. Security: I am no longer in danger of being bullied. My parents' business is flourishing.
5. Purpose: I am learning, developing and growing spiritually every day. I know that I am here on Earth for a reason. I may be here to make a difference. What that difference is I don't yet know, but I will find out!
6. Contribution: Somehow, my purpose will allow me to leave a lasting legacy, something that is beyond what I can learn at school. I don't know what it is, but there must be a reason why I have endured what I am enduring!
7. Creation: What will I create that my peers will appreciate me for? Will I invent something or act in a unique and unexpected way? Will that be my legacy?
8. Enjoyment: No matter what I am doing, I enjoy my work, study, friends and family, and I enjoy creating my legacy.
9. Prosperity: I am no longer worried about who is in competition with me. I form teams with people on a similar journey as we make our way into the future. We appreciate all that we have accumulated, materially and spiritually.

What are *your* values? Take some time to reflect on what is most important to you. You might like to make two lists: what your values are now (including 'negative' forms), and, where the less desirable ones are concerned, what you would prefer to have as your values. For example, right now you might be valuing privacy, autonomy and independence, and those values show up as you hiding away in your room, refusing to co-operate with others, and instead being a fierce loner. As you mature, those values might expand to include sharing, communication and making a contribution. (Or it could go the other way, from excessive giving to greater independence.)

Record your Current Values. Be as specific as possible.

Record your Ideal Values. Again, be as specific as possible.

4. Calibrate your energy

My old disempowering rule of listening to and believing my negative self-talk resulted in:

1. Low self-esteem
2. Lack of confidence
3. Lack of energy or motivation to participate in any activities that might contribute to my personal growth
4. Isolation
5. Frustration
6. Heightened anxiety
7. Debilitating depression
8. Hopelessness

All of these factors had led me into a 'downward emotional spiral'. If I had calibrated how I felt energy-wise, 0 being low on energy and 10 being high energy, here's how I would have measured myself in those eight areas:

1. Self-esteem: 2
2. Confidence: 3
3. Energy or motivation to participate in any activities contributing to personal growth: 3
4. Sense of Isolation: 7
5. Frustration: 7
6. Anxiety: 7

7. Depression: 9

8. Hopelessness: 9

How on earth was I supposed to become successful as a teenager if I were to continue pressing on with my old rules and the resultant low emotional energy?

My new rule of listening to the most empowering voice, whether internal or external, meant:

1. More control over my life (regardless of what my peers thought of me)
2. More energy into my true areas of interest
3. More interaction with like-minded people
4. Increased self-esteem
5. Increased confidence
6. Increased fulfilment
7. Increased contentment
8. Focusing on positive affirmations and disregarding negative ones.
9. Making plans for a happier future.

If I were to calibrate my energy levels for each of these now, here's what they would look like:

1. Control over my life: 9
2. Energy into my true areas of interest: 9
3. Interaction with like-minded people: 10
4. Self-esteem: 10
5. Confidence: 10
6. Fulfilment: 10
7. Contentment: 10
8. Focusing on positive affirmations and disregarding negative ones: 10
9. Making plans for the future: 10

This calibration exercise is a great way to identify the different energy levels associated with your old way of thinking and your new way of thinking. As you can see, those changes in my attitude gave me the energy to rebuild my life. You can't do anything when you're dead or incapacitated, but you sure can do something when *hope* fills you with energy. Hope gives you the will to deal with difficulties and do the things that will allow you to flourish.

Identify the emotional states and issues that have been making you feel drained and empty. Next to each state or issue, write down a number from 0-10 to calibrate where you feel your energy level stands.

Then write down what your new rules mean to you in terms of more energy, excitement, hope, or some other feelings. You might also like to calibrate those states.

When you compare your two lists, do you notice a change in the way you think? Does your ability to solve problems become more robust? Do you feel as if a weight has come off your shoulders? Does your new attitude warm your heart?

It became apparent to me, from the 'death' of the old David and the birth of the new, that new ideas and new dreams meant not only new hope but also much more energy. And hope, even in the form of a tiny seed inside a rotting dead piece of fruit, will eventually grow into a huge tree that can attract new life to it.

5. Manifest It!

To 'manifest' something is to demonstrate it, to make it a reality, to live it. Consider creating regular quiet moments to reflect and centre yourself and deliberately manifest your dreams. Some people closet themselves away in a room during their meditation period, maybe with a candle and a sheet of paper, and deliberately visualise themselves living the life of their dreams. They write this vision out or visualise it in full sensory detail, enjoying it and appreciating it as if it were happening right now.

The practice of meditation is invaluable in calming the mind. It is harder to rationalise a solution when your mind panics or is scrambled by fear, anger or depression. There are many different styles of meditation – you can meditate sitting in a room or walking in a field – but the main principle is to keep bringing your attention to a centre point, whether it is to your breath, to a candle or to a particular idea. The key is to find a still quiet centre.

So visualise yourself achieving your goals and dreams. *Make them happen.* Pursue what you want with full commitment.

6. Tips for Managing Relationships

- Find mentors, people you can trust who are demonstrating the ability to achieve what *you* want. They might be successful coaches, athletes, speakers, authors, business owners… Whatever their area of expertise, if you can't befriend them, hire them! There are many government and private organisations that can help you achieve your goals and dreams. For instance, just by looking online for a small business support group a few years ago, we discovered Family Business Australia, which turned out to be a great community and resource for us in resolving some disputes.

- Seek inspiration. There are also many free podcasts from all around the world in which inspiring individuals are interviewed, and there's always something to learn from these conversations. One of my favourite pastimes is watching videos of authors, psychologists, doctors and historians giving lectures and interviews. My personal library has doubled simply by listening to interviews given by authors promoting their latest book on a subject that piques my interest.

- But don't rely on other people to carry you through your life or sort out your problems for you. By all means, ask for help with your challenges or projects but don't expect your friends or the people you employ to do your work for you. Just as you can't expect to go to a gym, pay your membership dues, and then have the trainer at the gym do the work for you to get the results you desire, nobody can make decisions for you or do the work you need to do. If you want to have friends and be less lonely, you must align your behaviour with your goals and desires – e.g. take the risk of greater vulnerability by sharing your feelings rather than keeping your armour up and everyone out. Many people can advise you on how to deal with problems but in the end you must make your own decisions and wear the consequences of those decisions.

- Listen to those who have gone before you. Even if they appear to be old or old-fashioned, they have learnt some important lessons along the way.

- Be wary of the company you keep. You are likely to adopt the beliefs of the people you spend the most time with, so make sure the company you keep is in accordance with what you want in life. We can't choose our family but we can consciously choose our friends and associates, and through them, the beliefs we take on.

- Make sure you appreciate those who help you. It's a wonderful experience being helped, whether you've asked for the help or whether your helper saw you were down and offered support. By acknowledging those people who've had a hand in your rescue, you benefit and your helper feels good – a true win/win.

- Be there for others when it is their time of need. Helping others will do wonders for *your* self-esteem. However be wary of helping those who might not want your help. A line from the New Testament explains why: 'Do not cast your pearls before swine, lest they trample them under their feet and then turn and tear you to pieces.'

> "Helping one person might not change the whole world, but it could change the world for one person."
>
> – UNKNOWN

7. Some 'Growth' Strategies

- Develop emotional intelligence. Emotional intelligence means understanding and managing your feelings and being able to communicate effectively with the people around you so that you don't react unthinkingly. In blind states of anger and hatred we are unable to make rational decisions and may experience a costly aftermath. If you find yourself struggling with constant or repetitive frustration, aim to break that state so it doesn't control you. If you don't control a situation or state of mind, it rules you.

- Educate yourself. No matter how dire the situation you face, if you wish to push through and master your challenges, you must exercise your mind. Invest time in developing your mind just as you invest in your business, your career, your friends, your health or your personal wealth portfolio. Without control of your mind, those other investments are in danger of being damaged or lost. So read regularly. Consciously engage with the material you are reading. Cross-reference articles and build a reference library.

- Decide that your opinion of yourself matters more than others' opinions of you. If others like what they see in you, great! But if others belittle you, don't take their comments personally. Being dependent on other people's opinions is a sure recipe for disappointment. (They're not as 'cool' as they appear, so don't automatically view them as superior. Just because you weren't around when they made their mistakes doesn't mean they haven't made any.) Reminding yourself of this perspective is another way of exercising your mind.

- Be proud of your mistakes. Failure and mistakes are your best teachers. Each one offers opportunities for growth. Besides, nobody is flawless. We are not born as computers with software already installed; we are born as human beings who were designed to learn by trial and error..

> "The person who doesn't make mistakes is unlikely to make anything."
>
> – UNKNOWN

- Do the difficult. Keep doing your best, and more than that, do the difficult. A famous quote is that if you don't have a problem, get down on your knees and pray for one or you're not growing and might even be dead! So if you want to progress, do the difficult.

- Make a list of your strengths and then ask your four closest friends or relatives for their opinions about your strengths and what you would be great at. See what answers you get. You may be surprised at what you uncover!

> "Any man who starts with his liabilities before his assets is destined to have pain."
>
> – ANONYMOUS

- Summon the positive! Whenever you are feeling swamped by your old set of rules, think of the exact opposite scenario to what you are experiencing right now. You can't feel depressed when you're in a cheerful frame of mind. If you've been feeling anxious, direct your imagination toward the opposite scenario: see yourself in a scene that evokes calmness, security, tranquillity and peacefulness, or friendship, belonging, enjoyment and fun, and shared experiences.

You may choose to see yourself in the picture or *be* in the picture with the scene happening around you. Either way is fine. If you cannot picture this scene, feel it. If you cannot feel, smell it. For example, calmness may be represented by a perfumed candle in a quiet secluded room, or a field of green grass. Deliberately evoke the feelings you want to experience.

> "Positive thinking will let you do everything better than negative thinking will."
>
> – ZIG ZIGLAR

- Create an inspiring 'secret code'! The most empowering rule I made for myself when I was 12 is summed up by the acronym: IMAGINATION:

Investing IN
Many
Agreeable
Generous
Ideas
Novelties
And
Treasures
Including
Outstanding
Notions

That acronym might sound strange or absurd, but for some reason when I was 12 this combination of words thrilled and empowered me. It helped me to form a more open-minded, creative and resourceful attitude to life.

- Write a 'My Accomplishments' List

To those of you who have suffered deeply and feel you have only a depressing existence ahead of you, I offer this piece of advice: Write a list entitled, 'My Accomplishments In Life'.

Don't think that you don't have any accomplishments – you do, and probably more than you realise. You don't have to show this list to anyone, but recognising what you have achieved is empowering and useful.

We each have different accomplishments that relate to our values and goals and experiences. My list probably won't be relevant to you but I'm sharing it here in the hope that it triggers your thinking as you compile your list of accomplishments.

I have made peace with my school years.
I lost 25 kilos by committing to healthier habits!

I have my 10 friends from Kindergarten back, and the list continues to grow!

I flew over the school on my last day there as a demonstration of victory.

I've reconnected with Jo! Greatest of all: she is my friend, and fast becoming one of my closest friends.

I have regained my confidence when interacting with people after years of shyness and anxiety.

I competed in the Grand American Clay Target Shoot in Ohio.

I won three events in an Australian Dancesport Championship – all on the same day – and have partnered leading Australian dancers.

In the last 13 years, my dancing has improved at a PHENOMENAL RATE!!!

I flew a Spitfire over England! (This was a holiday adventure I had dreamed of as a kid. I'd never dared to believe I would ever actually experience it!)

I flew a DC3, a 1941 Tiger Moth and a Harvard. (Very ambitious flying dreams as these are very old rare aircraft – and now fulfilled!)

I flew in a glider.

I corresponded with Chuck Yeager, first man to officially break the sound barrier.

I made it to Disneyland!

I went to Egypt and explored all their great monuments, including a pyramid, Luxor, the Karnak Temples and Abu Simbel.

I am a recipient of the Red Cross 100 Donation Medal (for blood donations), which has gone a long way to fulfilling my personal need to contribute to society.

If you are struggling to list your accomplishments, start with the little things. Your list might begin like this:

- I can drive and have my own car.
- I am fit and healthy.
- I have a home.
- I have a family.
- I have friends.
- I can determine who I want in my life and who I don't want in my life.
- I can determine which activities are worthy of the limited time I have on Earth.

- I have the power to determine the course of my life and where to focus my energies. I can choose to pursue different interests if I want to.
- I can read and write.

Even if you don't have a family, you still have the capacity to meet new people and have them as friends. Many people feel closer to their friends than to their family, and you might feel like that too.

Even if you're not entirely healthy, you are probably not entirely sick – you might have a few ailments but be healthier than someone else you know.

Even if you don't own your own house or car, you probably have somewhere to live and some means of getting around, and you can be grateful for those.

The strategy I'm offering here is that even if you are struggling in the depths of despair and blocked by anger and frustration at your perceived circumstances, anchor yourself to something solid and build up from there. Even the smallest asset is a foundation you can build upon that will provide you with a sense of security.

As you list your accomplishments, visualise each one as a medal being pinned on your 'uniform'. People treat us as we treat ourselves, so when you treat yourself with respect and appreciation, you are more likely to receive that sort of treatment from others.

You might like to play the music that most inspires you while you compile your list. I was inspired to consider my accomplishments as medals after watching the movie *To Hell and Back* about Audie Murphy's experiences during World War II. The film finished by panning down and down and down over the magnificent decorations he had earned from his services during the war while a heroic march played in the background. The stirring music helped to build a sense of the significance of those medals.

Record what you have accomplished so far!

When you've completed your list, read over all the successes you've experienced in your life and *relive* each experience – how it looked, sounded, smelt, and felt.

If you don't feel inspired by your list, let mine be your catalyst for change. Tell yourself, *'If he can do it, I can do it! If he can have rich amazing experiences, so can I. He's no more special or worthy than me. I deserve to have a magnificent life too.'*

Record your answers to the following summarising questions regarding the content of this chapter.

1. How am I going to exercise my mind?
2. Which negative opinions of myself am I now rejecting?
3. Which 'mistakes' am I learning from, and what am I learning?
4. What are my strengths? (What are my friends' views of my strengths and possibilities?)
5. What is my pleasing 'opposite scenario'?
6. What is my acronym and what does it stand for?
7. What is my list of accomplishments?

My Vision.
Draw upon your responses to all the previous exercises to create a vision for your life and record it in as much detail as you can.

Then sit down with your new vision and make it yours! Own it! Tell yourself that you don't care what comes up to bite you! It can try to trip you up but you're going to get what you want anyway! This sort of resourcefulness is a prime skill to develop if you want to turn your life around.

I hope you will do these exercises conscientiously. Put your head down and start at the top with what makes YOU come alive, with YOUR bucket list, with your values and strengths... And then start manifesting!

It is encouraging that success breeds success, but don't rest on your laurels if you begin to succeed. Continue to strive in your personal education and development. These efforts will develop the 'metaphysical muscles' that will really count in your life. If you don't develop these, life will be much harder than it needs to be.

We don't live in a flawless world. We are all confronted by challenges from time to time, whether we want them or not. Challenges and support are the Yin and Yang of our existence and together they provide balance. All that can be expected of us is that we do our best.

Some challenges will seem insurmountable. No matter what you do, whose advice you follow, or who and what power you ally yourself with, you will not solve them. In those cases, when all else fails, I fall back on two rules I developed when playing computer games:

i) When you can't pass a level, hit the reset button and try again. If getting past this obstacle means the world to you, keep hitting the reset button. Reset! Reset! Reset! And train yourself to anticipate where your 'bogeyman' will come from next so that you can respond more effectively to your life challenges. Computer games become easier to play when you are the one who decides when to deal with the bogeyman, and how, rather than being on the back foot. The same applies to life in general.

ii) If you cannot pass the challenge, bypass it. Go around it and develop different skills for other problems you *can* solve until you are ready to deal with that one.

These are two elementary rules that can be applied to almost all challenges.

Your time on Earth is limited. You can't count on luck, so taking action on your goals is how you can maximise the possibility of experiencing 'magic' in your life.

NEW EMPOWERING RULE #23: Implement tried and true strategies for success.

"You don't have to be a fantastic hero to do certain things. You can be just an ordinary chap, sufficiently motivated to reach challenging goals."

– EDMUND HILLARY

"Success in life comes when you simply refuse to give up and when you have goals so compelling that obstacles, failure and loss only act as motivation."

– UNKNOWN

STRATEGIES FOR SUCCESS

David Gillman and Jacqui Clark, three times Australian Dance Sport Champions, 2011

David and Jacqui Clark, presentation of first event won, 2011

Dancing with Bronwyn Williams, 2015-2017

Angel on my shoulder

CHAPTER 14: The Rule Of Creative Competition And Reinventing Oneself

"Never compete; create."

– EARL NIGHTINGALE

After turning my life around, finding my life partner, travelling all over the world, becoming a five-times national Dancesport champion, reclaiming many friendships that should have been lost to time, and building a new house in a lovely rural area, do you think I had left my troubles behind? Or were all the lessons I'd learnt up to the age of 39 simply preparation for much worse?

I'd had a very hectic year in 2015. The Victorian Prison Industries, backed by the then reigning state government, had tried to implement a predatory pricing structure in the sash-printing industry. When we received word from some of our clients about how drastically Prison Industries was undercutting our prices, we were left scratching our heads. The last thing any small business needs is a David-and-Goliath struggle against its own government! The tax dollars we were providing to the government were being used against our business and other screen printers in the presentation awards industry because Prison Industries were exempt from paying award wages, sick leave, holiday pay, long-service leave, etc. since their workers were convict labour. In addition, their stock, ink, foil and machinery were all funded.

When we approached the government about this problem their answer was simply that they were providing the prison inmates with meaningful work, and that since the quality of their work was much lower than ours, they were inclined to price their products at a much lower rate. They didn't seem interested that their strategy put us in danger. They also didn't seem to care that if these inmates decided to start their own screen-printing businesses in the presentation ribbon industry after leaving prison, those ex-prisoners would also be struggling to compete against Prison Industries.

This wasn't the first time that the government-run screen-printing industry tried to pull the rug out from under us. One year, while representing the family business at the showgrounds, I walked past a show-dog exhibitor who was proudly displaying her ribbon. On closer inspection I noticed that one of our copyright scroll designs had been incorporated into the layout of the ribbon. When we challenged Prison Industries about this, they tried to claim that there was no evidence that the design was protected under copyright. It took four letters from our lawyer (and considerable expense) before they accepted that we were the legal owners of the design.

It just seemed so unfair! It was almost like school again. The bully (Prison Industries) was attempting to grind us out of business while the reigning headmaster (the government) appeared to be turning a blind eye to the whole problem!

The effect of this situation was that a good proportion of our customers were peeled off our books and we were faced with the challenge of keeping our doors open during a price war. As you can imagine, when a small business is up against a $2 billion giant that is being fed tax dollars, an unfavourable outcome is inevitable for the small business.

This time, however, my father and I created several new designs. Over the next three years we introduced three new body sash badges and two new printing scrolls. Printing scrolls are embellishment designs that are used to complement printed wording on a ribbon or body sash. As Prison Industries had previously demonstrated their inability or reluctance to recognise copyright laws, our family slapped copyright protection on everything that came off our 3D engraving pantograph machines.

We had to quickly update our marketing strategy and advise our remaining customers that our new designs were available. New colour catalogues with our latest designs were printed and sent out Australia-wide. Fortunately our remaining customers stayed and some that had gone to Prison Industries returned. Our business was saved but the cost to our family was enormous.

My family's worry that all our efforts in building our small business were to be destroyed took its toll on all of us. We were required to find ways to reduce costs, which meant that as staff left our factory we didn't replace them but instead looked for ways to automate our machines. I had never experienced levels of psychological and financial stress like this before, even when the so-called 'factory inspector' came to visit us in 1982. On top of that was the physical stress from working 12-14 hour shifts for months on end – and a quarter of that time I was alone in the factory.

With all the ribbon printing during the day, and the pantograph work at nights (after hours, at no extra wages), I was coming home later and later. This was quite dangerous as I was working in an area that was gradually being taken over by drug cultivators and dealers. I know this because the factories on either side of us were raided within two years of each other, a body had been found in a barrel in our street in 2009, and there were sporadic reports of people being shot outside their factories in our neighbourhood. By the end of 2015 this danger was constantly at the back of my mind. However, as the weeks turned into months, I became so tired that eventually I made a mistake. That mistake may have cost me my life.

One night I locked up the factory around 9:00 pm. With all that was weighing on my mind I was so tired that I was barely aware of my surroundings. But I did notice, as I walked wearily to my car, that the grass along the nature strip was really long. That was a snake risk for my dog and me so I brought my new iPhone out and took a couple of pictures of the long grass to send to the Council. Because it was dark, I used the flash feature. I was checking the quality of the photos on the screen as I headed back to the car when a voice behind me yelled:

"HEY, YOU! Hey, Arsehole! What are you doing taking pictures of my car?"

I looked back to the side of the road. A hotted-up car was following me and some young punk was leaning out of the driver's window waving a fist at me. I hadn't seen him or heard him when taking the pictures.

Drug busts were very common in the factories surrounding us so I was immediately on edge. I guessed that this young fellow must have been dealing but there was no way I could avoid him! He stopped his car and stormed out toward me. I noticed his girlfriend watching from inside the car.

"HEY! I'm talking to you! Did you take pictures of my car?! You know I can stab and shoot you for that, you c$%t!" With that, he shoved me so hard that I nearly crashed into the fence behind me.

How do you talk a young punk out of assaulting you when it's night-time and no-one is around? I had to keep my cool.

"Son, I didn't take pictures of your car. I didn't even know you were nearby."

"Bullshit! Do you have pictures of my car?"

He was right in my face. He was at least 3 centimetres taller than me and quite muscular. I calculated that even if he was unarmed, I only had a 40-50% chance of taking him on successfully. I pulled out my phone.

"Look, bud. Don't believe me? Take a look for yourself!" I showed him the iPhone screen.

He snatched my phone out of my hands and proceeded to scroll through my pictures. I waited nervously, then asked as sternly as I could: "Where is your car in those photos?"

"What are you taking pictures for at this time of night?" my aggressor asked in an irritated tone.

"Fella, do you see the long grass and the rubbish on the corner? I'm having to walk across that every day, worried that I or my dog is going to be bitten by a brown snake." I was feeling more and more irritated the longer he held me up out here.

"F%^ker! I don't care! There'd better not be pictures of my car on your phone!"

"Well, look closer, idiot!" I yelled.

"Give me your money, c%$t!" he demanded.

"I don't have any money. If I did, do you think I'd be working back so late!"

He looked back at my phone, flicking through my pictures.

My car was only eight feet away. I didn't rush, I just walked; I got into my car, closed the door and hit the lock. I started my car. He walked up and slammed the side panel of my car but didn't bother to try the handle. He turned and ran back to his car and took off. I tried to follow him to get a good look at his number plate but he was too quick. I gave chase for two kilometres but couldn't get close enough.

I filed a report about 20 minutes later with the police. I'd already contacted the phone company to deactivate the phone so he couldn't glean any more information from my address book. To my knowledge, he was never caught.

I was angry about that situation for a long time afterwards. It reminded me of the time I was bullied on the oval when 'Biff' decided to push me onto my backside. The value of this experience is that I had matured sufficiently that I was able to keep my cool and think through my options rather than reacting.

I suspect that if police officer Ben had reviewed the alternatives with me, we'd have arrived at these conclusions:

- Had I fought back in a physical way I might have been killed or permanently disabled, and if that had happened I would no longer be of use to my business and would have become a burden to my wife and other family members.

- Had I physically attacked and frightened off this fellow, I could have been locking up the factory three weeks later only to turn around and find myself surrounded by this robber and his fellow thugs. If I'd been murdered at this point, there was a good chance that my attackers would never have been caught.

- Had I totally lost my cool and run him over when I had the opportunity, the girlfriend witnessing from the passenger seat would have accused me of 'killing an innocent man for no reason', leaving me to be arrested and possibly sentenced. Even if I hadn't actually hurt him, there would be a good chance that I'd be put up on charges of threatening behaviour, even though he had threatened me first, simply because he had a witness on his side and I didn't.

I won in this instance because:

1. I kept my cool and didn't overreact.
I once heard a wise coach say that what matters is not what a person *does* to us but how we *interpret* the situation. Two people might experience being

threatened: one person reacts by lashing out and is injured, killed or sued; the other manages his or her emotions and is able to safely escape. Or, a more common example: two people might experience being criticised; one person decides that the comment is aggressive and feels hurt, defensive, angry, resentful… while the other takes a moment to process it and decides that it's actually useful feedback. This latter person feels momentarily embarrassed, perhaps, and then grateful.

2. I learnt a valuable lesson in 'situation awareness'.

Situation awareness is a term I came upon when reading about aviation. It means being aware of what is happening around us, comprehending what is happening, and responding appropriately. I lacked this awareness when that young fellow first showed up while I was taking photos, but once he spoke to me I paid lots of attention! I noticed what state he was in, what car he was driving, that he had a witness… Not noticing those things might have cost me my health or my life.

3. I lived through this near-assault, am unharmed and able to live my life fully and continue to contribute to society.

4. Having experienced this form of potential attack first-hand, I now contribute to charities that help other victims of crime and bullying.

OLD DISEMPOWERING RULE #15: Indulge in fear, resentment and anger.

NEW EMPOWERING RULE #24: Keep my cool and get creative.

CHAPTER 15: ReWriting The Rule Of The Jungle

"If opportunity doesn't knock... build a door."

– MILTON BERLE

I can still remember bank hold-ups and robberies being reported on the news at night during the 80s. I used to feel annoyed that these armed perpetrators would storm into a bank and order the teller to hand over all the money in their till or force the manager into the vault to unlock the safe – and get away with it! It seemed to take forever for the police to catch up with them, if they ever did. Eventually over the course of years, a tip-off might lead the police to the criminals. They would be tried and convicted, sent to jail for a certain number of years and then be released in the hope that they wouldn't commit the crime again.

Meanwhile, more news reports would appear with new criminals replacing old criminals. That cycle never ends. When people don't have constructive ways of solving their problems and meeting their needs they come up with illegal and destructive ways.

Bottom line, we all have one main need: to look after ourselves! It is a fundamental fact of nature – the law of the jungle – and also of human nature. In 1943 Abraham Maslow presented a model of the human psyche called 'the hierarchy of needs', and used the shape of a pyramid to illustrate those needs.

- Physiological needs such as food and water are the base essentials for a human to survive, and so they form the base of the pyramid.

- Once our survival needs have been met, we seek safety. In Western cultures today, safety manifests itself as the need for personal, financial and, of course, physical safety, which includes our health.

- Once our safety needs are met, we seek to feel love and belonging, so we look for friendships, intimacy and family.

- It is only after these basic needs are met that we can focus on fulfilling our 'higher needs', such as the need for self-esteem, acceptance, and respect from others.

- The penultimate layer of the pyramid relates to self-actualisation, or realising our full potential, which is when we achieve life goals, whether becoming a loving parent, guardian, mentor, inventor, etc. This level is where we go beyond the basics of daily life to the point where we are contributing to society.

- The peak of the pyramid is 'self-transcendence', when we have mastered all lower levels of human needs and now pursue and/or realise the higher goals of altruism and spirituality; it's where we act selflessly and focus on the wellbeing of others via practical forms such as philanthropy and volunteering, or simply by demonstrating kindness, compassion and generosity to others.

Not all of us attain this level of altruism during the course of our lives. Most of us are concerned with looking after ourselves and are not yet ready for the higher levels of existence. For example, many meat eaters, myself included, cannot turn down the offer of a chicken dinner or a nice Sunday roast lamb with gravy and vegetables. Even though we understand that an animal was sent to slaughter for the meat, we push this thought to the back of our minds as we smell the meat wafting through the air from the oven. We don't seem to care about the wellbeing of that animal because we are prioritising *our* desire to eat its meat. This is our fundamental self-interest at work.

Sadly, that self-interest can destroy families and businesses. When I was competing in the Grand American I made friends with a young man who was working for his parents in their family business. His mother was in control of the finances and general administration of the company, which wasn't doing very well. His father had cut this young man's wage to $100 a week and my friend was being asked to work without overtime pay. He agreed to this because he was convinced he was saving the business from going under – until he discovered that his mother was using her position to siphon money out of the business savings account and into her credit cards, and spending it on smart phone games, gambling and short jaunts to beauty parlours.

Meanwhile his depressed father was going insane from worry about financial stresses and the fear of divorce. When my friend confronted his mother, she did everything she could to prevent him and his father from accessing the online banking accounts.

In desperation, my friend sought help from a psychologist. He asked his parents to attend a meeting and they agreed, assuming that their son was having issues. When my friend confronted the financial issue and produced proof, his mother shook her head and denied everything while his father became even more deeply rooted in his depression. Nothing came of his effort to help, and my friend remained locked out of the business finances. He hired a business coach out of his own pocket but his parents were not receptive to changing what they were doing or receiving any help.

At the time he told me of this problem, I was not a qualified coach but I suggested one thing: "Get out of there! Restart your life!" He did, and he is much happier today.

As part of the school curriculum in my final year at high school, I attended the Holocaust Museum in Melbourne. Three survivors from Auschwitz were present that day and spoke to our group of their experiences. As it was 1993 they were in their mid-70s. Each speaker told a harrowing tale of survival and separation from family. One of the men described how he stood at the camp entrance as a young boy, clasping his father's hand and watching his mother and sister being escorted to a large hangar-like building, never to be seen again. He and his father were led to the other side of the camp to be transferred to a labour site to fuel the Nazi war machine. As many of us know, they were fed pitiful rations, worked ragged, and given very little sleep. If they dropped their production noticeably, they could be summarily shot or bayoneted in front of the other inmates.

Human history is full of stories like this, stories of slavery and cruelty where one group of 'expendable' people is exploited by another group that seeks to gain power of some form.

We each have a choice to stand by and watch or to help those people who are being unfairly treated, and while there seems to be a never-ending stream of media reports of human and animal cruelty, we will also readily find stories of people helping others, such as whenever there is a national crisis and homes are lost to flood or fire, or when people take in abused animals or homeless children. Even while the Nazis were committing atrocities during WWII, many Jewish families were being hidden, saved and protected by Polish and German families, and others throughout Europe.

So don't bury yourself in tragic events because that line of thinking and acting can darken your view of society. Aim for a balance: look after yourself and your needs (in ethical ways) so that you can flourish, *and* look for ways that you can help others. A simple act of kindness and helpfulness, especially when it is unexpected, is worth gold to someone in their hour of need. In that moment they feel that their existence might actually count for something after all.

If you find yourself feeling lost and uncertain and you cannot trust friends or family to guide you, enlist the help of a life coach. Life coaches are fast becoming a great go-to resource for helping people clear mental fog and achieve their goals. Coaches' problem-solving techniques often bring clients to solutions far more quickly than they might on their own or through reading a book. In many cases, the investment in a life coach can return many times what we pay for the sessions.

Life coaches draw upon a broad spectrum of strategies to help you focus on a solution to your problems. They are trained to not judge you and will methodically work with you through even the most apparently insurmountable problems. They won't wave a magic wand and pronounce you instantly cured, but they can nudge you toward your own solutions and keep you accountable in following through with them. Coaches specialise in a range of fields, such as business, finance, fitness and health. I have found that several of my dance sport teachers also make good life coaches. This makes sense because the principles of success can often be transferred from one area to another.

Having a life coach is a great, practical way to analyse and deal with your challenges. Even though I'm a registered life coach, I call upon the services of a fellow coach when I'm stuck in annoyance and frustration. Here's an example from a session with my master coach, R!k Schnabel.

In 2015, after years of competing in the world of ballroom dancing, I had decided I wanted to become a dance teacher myself. But in order to do this, I felt that I needed to expand my teaching skills and understanding of human nature. I decided that life coaching would be the key to improving myself. After reviewing many life-coaching courses, I didn't know which way to turn. I raised the subject one day in a meeting with a financial adviser, and she mentioned that her fiancé had just completed a course with a life coach called R!k Schnabel, whose fees were very reasonable.

When I called R!k's office I expected to get a sales pitch from a secretary and a payment plan. Instead, R!k himself answered the phone. The phone call must have gone for half an hour, during which R!k patiently listened to my life story. By the time we had finished speaking I was sold! I started a payment plan that June for a first course that would begin in November. And then disaster struck. On October 18 at 6:30 a.m. my wife nudged me awake, saying, "David, your Mum's on the phone."

It turned out that our factory has been damaged in a firebombing and my parents had already been interviewed on national television.

I rolled out of bed, dazed. Of all the strategies that certain parties had used to push us out of business during the last 45 years, this new development might have succeeded – permanently!

I grabbed the remote and waited for the 7 a.m. news broadcast. Sure enough, there were my parents being interviewed on national television. At that moment I imagined that everything we had put into that factory was lost. Our stock had been damaged by water the Metropolitan Fire Brigade used to stop the fire from entering our factory – everything was damaged or destroyed! Our clientele would have no reason to stay with us. I imagined our opposition rubbing their hands together, making sure their office staff were quick to answer panicked phone calls from our clients who needed their orders filled.

Our family was left dumbstruck. All seemed lost. My mind quickly ran over contingency plans to keep my income flowing. I had two mortgages, one on my home and another on a recently acquired investment property. On top of all that, I was five months into my payment plan with R!k. I had to make a call. Maybe I could request a hold on my payments until such time as I could find another job and then resume my course. After a frantic email to R!k, he called back. I told him everything that had happened and expressed my concern that my wages might be cut off. R!k listened patiently until I finished. Then he said something that I will never forget:

"David, you know that in times like these there's nothing like a cleansing fire to start over."

I didn't need to hear those words again. I knew exactly what he meant. He coached me to acknowledge what had happened and then leave the feelings of hopelessness and despair behind; they weren't going to serve me in to the future. I needed to keep focused on what life coaching could bring me: a new vocation. Those words of encouragement from R!k were all I required to keep pressing on. He had me convinced that no firebombing bogan or factory inspector was going to undermine my success in life!

A few days later, my parents decided to buy a new factory. They had received enough phone calls and emails from concerned clients that they were encouraged to reopen. My wages weren't stopped as we had sufficient money owing from our clientèle to keep us paid and fed.

I attended R!k's class in November as planned. It was one of the most illuminating educations I ever had! After the semester was completed, I was handed my certificate of graduation – I was now qualified as a coach. But I still doubted myself. We had learnt so much during those weeks that my mind was swimming in information. How could I incorporate what I now knew in the dance coaching I gave my students?

I was given the opportunity in the following month when two students approached me just minutes before they were to dance their final year exam dances. Both were feeling nervous. The training I had received from R!k's classes helped me to notice *how* they were causing their own anxiety: their breathing was short and quick and they were frightening themselves with the idea that they wouldn't remember the figures they needed to dance during the exam.

The knowledge of how to help them kicked in so automatically that I couldn't believe it. To begin with, I was able to easily establish rapport with them. Rapport is a deep sense of comfort and connection. It is one of the primary lessons in NLP and the essential precursor for achieving any kind of therapeutic intervention. I asked them to follow me to a quiet area at the back of the church hall where the exam was being held. There I asked them to match my breathing. I slowed my breathing down until it became deep and relaxed; gradually their racy, shallow breathing calmed down too. Then I began to speak to them in the hypnotic tones that NLP practitioners use to deliver empowering messages.

"You know these dances," I said. "You have practised them so often that you know how to dance the figures automatically…"

After a few minutes they were totally relaxed. I finished with an upbeat, encouraging message: "Now go out there and show everyone in this school what you can do! This is your time to shine!"

I made sure they knew I was watching them as they danced their exam routines. Both students were awarded Honours. Afterward they came and thanked me for my help. I walked away, grateful and realising that I was now more than just a dance teacher and 'printer of ribbons'. I was truly a coach. I felt as powerful as if I had a telekinetic power!

If a student had asked me for advice before I had done the life coaching course I am certain that I would have turned around to them and *commanded* them to remember their training! In other words, "Get Over It!" That is of so little help to people who are experiencing acute anxiety that it is next to no use. Messages like that certainly didn't help my frail self-esteem at various times during my school years.

In hindsight I am certain that few of my schoolteachers had been taught to *coach*. They had been trained to deliver information, but not to work with anxious students (An exception was John Weedon). Would it have changed my life if more of my teachers had received that sort of personal development training? I'm sure of it! Could the damage to my early life have been prevented? I imagine so. Would I have become the person I am today? Naturally I would have developed differently with different inputs. I do know that I was fortunate in having been able to intuitively coach myself at crucial times in my childhood, and that others such as my father stepped in to help me. In each stage of my life some form of coaching has been essential.

Overcoming challenges can make us stronger but a relentless stream of challenges can crush us if we don't receive the right support or give ourselves the right encouragement – the choice to meet our needs is ours.

OLD DISEMPOWERING RULE #16: Feel swamped by external events.

NEW EMPOWERING RULE #25: Don't bury myself in tragic events outside my range of influence.

It is good to be aware of such events but it burns your energy to dwell on situations you cannot change.

NEW EMPOWERING RULE #26: Surround myself with like-minded people.

If your current friends or even family don't suit you or can't help you, find new allies with similar needs to yours. (Do your best not to alienate your friends and family in the process).

NEW EMPOWERING RULE #27: Invest in a life coach.

Life coaches are as important to your growth as a property investment is to your financial future. Invest in yourself by looking for the best coach you can find. You may find that the outcome is aspirations and achievements far higher than you can right now possibly imagine!

"Never, never, never give up!"

– WINSTON CHURCHILL

"When you feel that you have reached the end and that you cannot go one step further, when life seems to be drained of all purpose – what a wonderful opportunity to start all over again, to turn over a new page."

– EILEEN CADDY

CHAPTER 16: New Rule: Appreciate Hurtful Experiences

"Never to suffer would have been never to have been blessed."

– EDGAR ALLAN POE

Can you imagine standing in front of an audience of your peers and, for the first time ever, publicly speaking about your most private shame and how you overcame it?

This is what I found myself doing in July 2017. I was in my third semester of Life Coaching with R!k Schnabel. This time I was enrolled in a course called 'Speaking With Confidence'. Out of the three courses so far, this was the most fun but also especially useful for those dealing with the very common phobia of public speaking.

One particular day we were asked to be the worst audience imaginable! Each student would name his or her deepest fears about becoming a public speaker; then we, the audience, were to act out those fears. We could be totally obnoxious, rude, sexist, racist – the purpose being to challenge our fellow participant so that he could learn to deal with hecklers in a controlled and safe environment. The speaker was supported by a coach throughout this experience, and at the end of the exercise there was a group hug for all so that no misunderstandings occurred between the students.

We had been asked to announce the topic of our graduation speech in a 10-minute presentation, and had to utilise the tools we had learnt during our NLP training. The topics my peers presented ranged from volunteer work at overseas charities, to resisting the addiction of social media, to a new cleaning machine at a very affordable price, to a new means of self-exploration and development.

I had intended to speak about Aerial Combat Tactics in World War II, and how the lessons developed from those tactics could be applied to the modern day. But then my mind flashed to something funnier: what if I spoke about the benefits of my world famous 'Armpit Special'?

The Armpit Special is a term coined by one of my friends. When I was working in the factory for my parents, I would occasionally turn into 'Lunch Boy' by donning my cap and heading out in my 1977 Chrysler Valiant to pick up lunches for everyone. Occasionally I'd pass a factory that looked like any other sandwich shop. It was called 'The Hot Spot' and had a great neon sign with flames on top of the word 'HOT'. I figured that the burgers in there would probably be pretty good, but the black gates to their driveway were always closed, which was peculiar for a sandwich shop at 12:30 in the afternoon. One day I asked my friend Jon what the story was with this café.

Jon cracked up laughing. "Dave," he said, "that place is a brothel! What were you hoping to get for $10.00 there? If you're lucky you might get an Armpit Special but that's about it!"

At that time, I was living in a unit in Ascot Vale and I was looking for a name to personalise my sweet and sour chicken dish. I got over my embarrassment about not realising The Hot Spot was a brothel, and instead took advantage of Jon's humour and named my dish an 'Armpit Special'. To this day, when visiting relatives and friends around the world, the David Gillman Armpit Special is always prepared as a thank you for having me over to visit!

It seemed like a great idea for my speech. Everyone else's sounded so serious and mine had the potential to be quite a comedy act. However as the students stood up to announce their subjects, my mind began to race and something in the back of my mind screamed out to be heard. When R!k faced me with his "What will your speech be?" I only paused for a moment before saying, "'Triumph Over Isolation', R!k."

I immediately felt the energy of several sets of eyes focusing on me with curiosity, and realised that I had sounded quite emotional when I spoke.

"So what will your speech cover?" R!k asked.

"The challenges and isolation I faced when I was young, and an idea I developed for how to overcome those problems." My voice was wavering slightly.

R!k responded that the topic sounded intriguing but he detected some emotional charge in my voice so he suggested that I get some coaching from my fellow student to handle the charge before the time came to deliver my speech.

I slumped back in my seat. Everyone else seemed to be so happy and in control as they announced their topic. I felt I had let myself down. I began to second-guess myself – maybe this was not the right topic for me? Maybe I wasn't ready to talk about that period of my life… Because, much as I felt that I'd overcome my troublesome past ages ago, I suspected that if I had to get up on stage and speak about this period of my life, I would discover some feelings that were still quite raw.

I figured that if I was to move on and help others who'd experienced similar things then it was going to be vital that I not only own the situation but be able to speak freely about it. Falling apart publicly on this topic was not going to be acceptable, especially as I was now a Master Life Coach practitioner! The seriousness of the course brought home to me that my experience of overcoming isolation and attempted suicide was an important issue, and so it was especially important that I be able to talk about it publicly, without worrying about how my audience was judging me.

All challenges present opportunities for growth! You can't coach someone on something that you have an emotional charge on; you have to clear your own charge first. In my case, the effect of that charge was something akin to Post Traumatic Stress Syndrome. Even after spending thousands of dollars on months of coaching and NLP training, I still had the remnants of emotional reaction to those years and that issue. *How do you clear an emotional charge that someone has been carrying for nearly 30 years?*

As we ended the lesson for the day, my coaching buddy, Duane Brown, came up to me and asked if I wanted to do some coaching with him to settle the emotional charge. I agreed and we made time to work on the problem the following night.

When we got together, Duane asked if I could give the emotional charge related to my graduation topic an 'intensity score' from 0 = feeling miserable, to 10 = feeling great. I answered, "Three". I had never spoken openly about the day I nearly took my life with someone I'd only known for a matter of weeks.

I had only told my wife, Viv, and a few close friends (including Jo), but I was committed to getting that emotional charge out of my voice so I told him the story.

Duane then asked me to relax, close my eyes and listen to his voice as he guided me through a meditation and 'Timeline exercise'. Timeline Therapy is an exercise done in your imagination in which you 'leave' present time and go into your past. You sit in an imaginary theatre and, one by one, you invite all those who have caused you pain and grief in the past onto the stage so you can forgive them.

Duane guided me into a deeply relaxed state until I could easily visualise the stage and those particular people, but as I called them onto the stage I found that I couldn't forgive them. I could see them, I could *tell* each individual that I forgave him or her, but it was an empty statement; I didn't feel as if I were really forgiving them at all.

The trouble was that while I was still consciously aware that my mind was now in the body of a 41-year-old, all the events that each person represented seemed to be so ingrained that I couldn't hit that reset button! It felt to me as if each of those people was looking down his nose at me from the stage with a sardonic smirk, as if to say, "Tough luck, Gillie! Live with it! Too bad! You're not going to be able to undo what I did to you! I got to you and there's nothing you can do about it now!"

And as all the characters smirked at me and even joked about how they had got to me and damaged me, one final scene played out: me sitting on the couch with that gun in my hands.

I was struck by the realisation that I was still thinking about those characters as 'mongrels'. My speech would be a form of revenge – I would be able to shame those people who had hurt me in the past. Essentially, I was still holding a grudge.

My mistake was compounded by the fact that I had ignored the lessons I had arrived at earlier in my life. My suicide attempt at age 12 might have been well and truly over, but I was still holding onto grudges and they were still having a damaging effect on me.

The realisation that day in the locker room with 'Biff' that revenge by physical violence was going to lead to a no-hope existence had held me back from my knee-jerk plan of belting him over the head with my hockey stick. But the hunger to do it was still there because in my eyes he'd escaped with his unacceptable treatment of me.

My friendship with Jo had been restored and was in a better state than ever before; however, the image of her walking away with that boy during 'Jump Rope For Heart' Day in Year 6 was still haunting me. I had been so upset that I'd made no further attempts to talk to Jo from that day until our paths crossed much later in our lives. Watching her with him had sent my self-esteem plummeting to such a degree that it felt like a boulder was crashing through my mind, heart and guts. My school marks fell to borderline C's and D's and even F's. My physical fitness diminished and my lack of energy was apparent to everyone around me. My stubborn childhood belief that I would end up with one of my childhood crushes tripped me up profoundly.

I am pretty confident that my career suffered as a result of all the attacks and disapointment. When I started getting my life together in my 20s, I had to make up a lot of lost ground in education and self-esteem. If I'd had the mental and emotional clarity and space to study, I would have done better in those final exams and then had more vocational options. My inexhaustible interest in early aviation combat had driven a desire to become a pilot who flew old warbirds at air shows, not a printer who spent half his time working on his own before leaving in the early hours of the morning when he was easy prey for muggers.

Finally, as every character on that stage summoned a memory of one or more painful events, I realised that my biggest mistake had been focusing on my anger and frustration and my ongoing desire to somehow get back at them (despite the period having long since passed), rather than creating room for forgiveness or understanding of each event, of the perpetrators and of myself. *I* had decided which feelings to allocate to each event. *I* had decided to play and replay these moments over and over again in the same old mindset of resentment. In short, they were still beating me because I was allowing my memory to do it!

My belief was that these accumulated incidents could not be changed.

151

They were set in stone and, unlike Marty McFly in *Back To The Future*, I couldn't go back to those events and subtly change the environment to protect my younger self or allow him to come out of each situation unscathed. This was the root of my frustration. No reset button to hit!

As their sardonic faces grinned at me from 'on stage' and they waited to see how many more times I would allow their memory to beat me up, I asked myself how I could turn this situation around and use their memory *in my service* and not against me.

Then it hit me. I was looking for a solid hard core solution in the here and now; the graduation speech for the ending of my course provided that opportunity.

Just as that thought entered my mind, Duane brought me out of the 'stage room' and back into the present. I opened my eyes and he asked me to give another score out of 10 to calibrate how I was feeling now. I was still a 'three'. Sensing that Duane might start doubting his ability to coach me, I felt that I had to supply an explanation for the lack of change.

I explained that at the age of 12 I had felt that I couldn't speak about my problems for fear of being ridiculed, and perhaps my 'code of silence' was working against me. I suggested to Duane that we try the exercise again, but this time I would describe what was going on aloud rather than just doing the process in my mind. In that way I was conquering my old habit of staying silent.

So back into the meditation and back into the past I went. And this time I really began to feel it! The old intensity, the trauma, sadness, despair and depression began to bubble up again. I described my anxious childhood and the bullying at school and that terrible day at my house when I was 12.

They were standing there in front of me. Some of them, like 'Biff', were now taunting me, even miming how they had heroically shoved me on my backside, burnt my hair with cigarette lighters, tripped me in the locker area… They were carrying on like monkeys. I watched them, thinking…

'Yeah, you bastards got me back then. I'm sure you were all feeling very brave when you attacked me in the ways you did. And I'm sure you are right now recalling how you got it over old Gillies, how you got away to brag about it to your friends and even your families.'

Recalling that I was now a 41-year-old successful adult only a few days away from graduation, and that my future as a coach was waiting for me, I continued to process...

'I can't beat you in the past to be sure. But I can bring you into the present on my terms, and I can continue to use you as examples into the future if my coaching requires it.'

At that moment, 'the stage' became quiet. Some of the sardonic smirks disappeared, while other faces began expressing confusion and annoyance.

'You might be untouchable in the past,' I said, *'but you are now all my instruments in the present and into the future.'*

Then I chose to play a memory on the screen behind these characters. It was the rumpus room again. But this time I was putting the gun away. I was walking back down the hallway and into my dishevelled bedroom.

'The fact is, guys, I'm resilient. You taught me to be this way. That sullen boy survived and is now about to start coaching children, teenagers and maybe even your peers at work on how to overcome people like you.'

My first headmaster stood out from the crowd. *'If you're going to do this talk and be who you say you're going to be,'* he warned, *'you're going to have to admit all the shame you felt at our hands.'*

In my mind, I walked up to the stage and beckoned him to come closer, as if I was going to share a secret with him.

'So be it!' I said. *'That kid you tormented is holding hope for thousands of others, and you helped make that possible!'*

With that, Duane once again talked me out of the 'stage room'. I had derailed my suicide that day in 1988 and the lesson I was bringing back from the experience was not how to forgive those characters, but how I was to get on with my life. All I had to do was to forgive *myself*, because the key issue to the emotional charge in the present was understanding that keeping past events alive in my mind had compounded them.

The concern that I would not do well in my speech, coupled with the need to build my authority through public speaking, were the impetus for me to finally completely tackle this emotional roadblock. No more would I be concerned about the judging eyes of the audience or anyone else's opinion.

Those times had passed and this was what I'd made of the situation. I was to be there for the audience. My story was merely required as proof that one could survive that type of trauma.

In order to complete this Timeline Therapy exercise, Duane asked me to indicate an anchor so that when I was ready, he could lead me out of it safely and I would be able to bring with me the knowledge that I'd overcome the experience. My anchor was to be a click of my fingers.

At his command, I pictured myself outside of the stage room. I looked behind me. It was an old brick building, tin roof, dusty windows, an old cracked concrete footpath with spindly weeds growing out of it. I reached into my pocket, pulling out an old walky-talky. I brought the device up to my mouth and uttered, *'Burn it!'*

A few moments later, the roar of a single engine Dauntless dive-bomber flew low over the building. Under its belly hung a huge napalm bomb. Anticipating the exact moment, I snapped my fingers as the bomb dropped. The theatre exploded and then erupted in flame, and I was free.

I didn't admit this scene to Duane. As far as he was concerned, I was simply floating up and above the stage as per his directions and heading back towards the present. But for me, the visualisation of burning the building down and blowing it up was my most powerful means of destroying an old unhelpful anchor to the past. It didn't concern me that Duane was following the script while I was experiencing something completely different. What had to be done, was done…

The lesson I learnt from those experiences, which is what is now coming through in this book, was to consciously choose how I was interpreting my life experiences and to create empowering personal life 'rules' rather than just reacting to my life experiences. My intention in sharing my challenges and breakthroughs is to offer hope to those going through experiences like mine. I want to coach people who have suffered and help them deal with their buried skeletons so that they, in turn, can help themselves and others.

When we recalibrated how I was feeling at the end of this second exercise, it was a nine out of 10. I was still a bit tearful, but now I was ready to address my audience without the emotional charge.

I'm grateful that I trusted my impulse to talk through the process rather than doing it in my mind. Answers from within are the best as they are particularly tuned to the client's problem and come from his or her own mind, heart and gut rather than from the coach's perspective.

Graduation Day arrived and I felt quite nervy, but it was a different type of nerviness – more of an excitement than anxiety or emotional charge. Duane patted me on the back just before I walked on stage – a very helpful anchor! The music that would introduce my presentation was 'Victorious' from the movie, *The Untouchables*. As the music faded, the nerves disappeared and I took everyone on a journey with me…

My speech went well. I managed to describe my experience without burying either myself or the audience in the most upsetting moments from my past. I finished with a few images from my wedding, which symbolised my triumph over isolation. Later I discovered that my message of hope had resonated with the audience, and that fact on its own cancelled out the pain of the past. From now on, instead of being buried by my past I would use negative attitudes toward me as my power source to inspire others.

It has been quite a journey… I hope that my story will inspire you to keep getting up, no matter how many times you trip or feel as if you are failing. If others only seem to have themselves in mind and want you to serve their purposes, look for a way to escape that trap and create your own happiness and fulfilment. To use my trusty metaphor and strategy: when playing a computer game that is too hard to master in the beginning, it's smart to reset the level to an easier setting until you have gained some skills. Find someone who can train you to overcome your problems. Find out what it is that keeps you from having a crack at your dreams. Don't settle for the dregs of life; take control of your life and your surroundings! ReWrite the Rules of Your Life. Then pass on what you've learnt.

OLD DISEMPOWERING RULE #17: Resent past hurtful experiences.

NEW EMPOWERING RULE #28: Appreciate those experiences. Learn the lessons.

"Our lives begin to end the day we become silent about things that matter."

– MARTIN LUTHER KING JR.

"Go for it. No matter how it ends. It was an experience."

– UNKNOWN

CHAPTER 17: Apologies And The Forgiveness Process

"When you forgive, you in no way change the past – but you sure do change the future."

– BERNARD MELTZER

During Fourth Grade a new boy to the school had taken an interest in messing with me. During art class, he'd simply walk up to my desk and take my pencils, glue and ruler without asking – and not give them back. At the end of each class I had to grab them from him. Being only nine, my patience quickly wore thin. One day 'John' took some pencils from my pencil case and 'accidentally' bumped me as he turned away. His friends on the other side of the table were watching and chuckling.

I snapped!

Teeth gritted, fists gripped, I charged after him and flung my foot right up his backside! Unfortunately, as my foot connected, I slipped on the lino floor and down I went – on *my* backside. The thud could be heard all around the classroom, and the other students erupted in laughter. I went to get up and have another go at the new boy but as I did the art teacher grabbed me by the arm and dragged me to his office.

In tears of frustration I explained what had been going on. Our teacher brought John in and forced us to apologise to each other. John didn't take long to apologise but it took something like ten minutes of coercion and threats from the teacher that we weren't leaving his office until there was an apology from me. Begrudgingly, I gave mine and we left, late for our next lesson.

Until that day I had never been *forced* to apologise. If I apologised, it came genuinely and naturally from me because I had wronged the other party or accidentally hurt them when they hadn't done anything to warrant it. I had no problem with apologising in those cases. But this apology under duress muddied the idea for me. It now meant that I could be forced to apologise to someone who had humiliated or even assaulted me even when I was initially minding my own business and their attack on me had been completely unprovoked.

I formed a rule from this day: *"If forced to apologise under duress, I will only feign it. I will not have anyone tell me what to think or believe!"*

This rule became a pattern that I followed for many decades. It served me well, or at least, I believed it did. Unfortunately, following this rule came at a cost because I would resent that forced apology, and the problem with resentment is that your mind burns a lot of energy as you continually think how unfair it was and how you are going to get your sweet revenge! Not only are you constantly simmering with anger about this unresolved issue, but your preoccupation with it distracts you from more worthwhile goals, from your studies, and perhaps even from sleep. In essence, whoever you perceive got to you is still messing with you, and they're not even there! The longer this goes on, the more destructive it becomes.

It was during R!k's 'Speaking With Confidence' course that I discovered a very profound piece of wisdom:

> "Resentment is like drinking poison and then hoping it will kill your enemies."
>
> – NELSON MANDELA

There are many different versions of this profound idea about revenge, resentment and anger, but they all lead to the same conclusion: hold onto resentment or a grudge, and you slowly poison your own life (and your own body). You will recall from Chapter 7 that as I became drunk on revenge and retribution, I was simultaneously in danger of becoming sociopathic. My attitude nearly ruined my life, not to mention Biff's. Writing this book and assisting others who may be facing similar issues is a far more constructive way of responding to bullying and similar attacks than revenge or resentment.

There is another way of dealing with a long-standing grudge, and that is to forgive. A 'Forgiveness Strategy' is a series of steps that take you from resentment to acceptance and peace.

Why have a forgiveness strategy? A forgiveness strategy enables you to tackle an unresolved issue that has been looping over and over and distracting you from your priorities, your dreams and your goals. It shifts you from helplessness and victim-consciousness to a resourceful empowered mindset.

The Forgiveness Strategy

Since time machines are yet to be invented we can't physically go back in time to prevent certain events in our lives from occurring, but the founders of NLP have created a strategy that enables us to change our perception of past events so they no longer trouble us as they used to. The effect of this strategy is as if we 'went back in time'.

I used a Forgiveness Process in conjunction with Timeline Therapy (described in Chapter 16). Here is the step-by-step method you can use.

Step #1. Come up with a strong enough reason to forgive.

Understand that nobody can force you to forgive someone who has treated you unfairly. But if you have unwillingly spoken the words 'I forgive you', eventually you will require peace of mind, and that's where true forgiveness comes in.

The process of forgiveness is not necessarily about forgiving the other party for all their wrongs and injustices towards you; *it is about taking back your power over what you want to experience.* You can't go back in time to undo the damage of what they said or did. Instead, you must look deep inside yourself and fully acknowledge that **you** are playing the memory of this injustice over and over again. They attacked you once, but *you* have been keeping the pain and resentment alive. Once you understand this, you have determined that you are in charge of your life experience and the other party has no more influence over you.

Step #2. Identify what the problem is *really* about, and how it is blocking you from moving forward and living a more fulfilled life.

Which are the old rules or beliefs that are holding you back? Write your answers to whichever of the following questions apply to you on a separate sheet of paper[6]:

- a) What is the real problem here? *(E.g. 'I can't get on with my life because this issue is constantly frustrating me', or 'This issue is making me angry/frustrated/isolated/depressed'.)*
- b) Why can't I trust anyone?
- c) Why am I discouraging myself from pursuing my original dreams and aspirations?
- d) When did I hand my power over to this past event?
- e) Is this mostly about me losing face?
- f) How much time am I losing every day, week, month or year?
- g) How much more of my limited time am I willing to spend reliving this problem and surrendering my power to something that doesn't exist anymore?
- h) Which old rules and beliefs are holding me back?

Step #3. Decide that 'What's done is done.'

Once you have determined that it doesn't serve you to keep replaying the same old memory, write that memory on a separate piece of paper and say aloud, 'What's done is done!' Then ask yourself…

Step #4. How can I build or re-build from this chapter in my life?

Think about what you really want in your life. Know that you cannot go back in time and that everything you do from this moment on is for you and those people who matter to you.

If you are ready to choose to be deliberately creative in regard to your life, write down your answers to these questions:

- a) If I can't change the past, what can I use of it to make a better life for me now and into the future?

---

6   I.e. Not in your notebook.

b) What resources do I have?
c) What resources can I create?
d) Who can help me?
e) Would changing my location be 'the difference that makes the difference'?
f) How can I use the negative influences in my life in a positive way?

By reflecting on questions like these, you will begin to empower yourself to change your mindset from a reactive self-pity mindset to a constructive, resourceful, problem-solving mindset that gives you your power back, no matter what any other party tried to do to you in the past. (For points 2-6, write down specific dates by which you will action those points so they are not vague floating ideas but actual plans of action).

Another useful strategy is to create a vision board, as mentioned in Chapter 13. (These can also be created on a computer or smart device.) Remember that it's usually wise to keep your vision board private. You don't want comments from friends or family members who might not understand what you are endeavouring to do.

Remember that pain can be good motivation, and being fed up with pain is excellent leverage for you to make a constructive shift.

Step #5. Decide that the bully/antagonist of your past is now confined to the past.

In the previous chapter I imagined that all my antagonists were standing up on stage in front of me, carrying on like monkeys and pretending to re-enact how they had 'heroically' messed with me. My big insight from that Timeline exercise was realising I couldn't stop them in the past and couldn't get back at them in the past, but I could use my memory of them to coach others in the present and into the future. Before the 'Speaking With Confidence' course, it hadn't occurred to me that I had to undergo a forgiveness process until it came time for the speech. The speech helped me discover my reason, my *'Must'*, for leaving that stage and walking out onto my own stage as the owner of all my experiences and an inspirer of others.

In my case, the Forgiveness Process was about me, not them. Realising that I had learnt from and overcome each confronting experience – the factory inspector, the bullies at school, those particular teachers who seemed apathetic to my troubles, the mugger outside my factory, the factory fire – helped me to see that they were no longer the problem; the problem had become my habit of staying attached to an old story, of keeping alive old grievances. But that problem was no longer relevant. *I was still here! Alive! Married! Friends everywhere! I had rescued others from their despair!* Those antagonists were no longer calling the shots.

The requirement to give a speech triggered the process I needed to go through in order to be able to coach other people in truly constructive ways.

So, how do you forgive yourself for keeping old memories alive? By deciding how you can best use those memories to help yourself and the most important others in your life.

Answer these questions in your notebook:

a) How are *your* old stories affecting your current quality of life? Is what you're making of your old stories serving you or holding you back?

b) How might your new stories or vision affect your quality of life now and into the future?

c) Where might your new life take you once you've shed all your old disabling stories? *(E.g. A new part of the world? A new society or club? Working in a new career?)*

d) How might the people in your most desirable environment be treating you?

e) What actions can you now take to ensure this will become your new story?

Evaluate and list the difference between your new insights and the old hate/revenge program that used to loop over in your mind.

Rate them by impact. Give your resentful/angry old beliefs a score out of 10, and then give your empowered beliefs a score out of 10.

Step #6. Follow up with *ACTION!*

Your actions determine your results. You can make all the plans you want but without *taking action on those new ideas*, you will remain stuck, particularly if you choose to hold onto old beliefs, rules and strategies. In an action plan the first step is of particular importance, especially if your new plan requires multiple steps. So what is the *first most important action* you can take?

After taking that first step, what is the next most important step? Using a divide and conquer strategy, take one step at a time and you will end up where you want to be.

List your First Action Steps in your notebook.

Step #7. Burning Your Bridges

After completing all of the above steps, take the sheet of paper on which you wrote your non-serving memory in the 2nd and 3rd Steps of the Forgiveness Process and tear them up, shred them or burn them as a symbolic act that represents completing with the past.

Commit to reading your answers to Step #5 first thing after you wake up in the morning and last thing before you go to sleep at night. If you are able, take some time to contemplate your answers. Visualise living your dreams and thoroughly enjoying your new life. Visualise your most important cherished dreams over and over again. Keeping your focus on what is important to you ensures the success of this Forgiveness Process.

If you need help, please reach out to me. My contact details are at the end of this book.

OLD DISEMPOWERING RULE #18: If forced to forgive, I will only feign it. I will not have anyone tell me what to think or believe!

NEW EMPOWERING RULE #29: If forced to forgive, deeply consider how it serves me to forgive. Remember that my resentment poisons *me*, not the other person.

Dwelling on the past, especially when you experienced hardship from someone who wronged you, keeps you stuck there. You cannot undo the past, but you can rewrite your interpretations of the past and build your future the way you want it.

"Holding onto anger is like drinking poison and expecting the other person to die."

– BUDDHA

CHAPTER 18: Support Systems

It is such a great support to have a mentor, especially when it turns out that those who were supposed to guide us did not, in the end, have skills equal to the task.

That's the beauty of working with a coach. Coaches are trained to listen carefully and advise in a constructive way. The world needs more coaches like Kerrie and R!k, and the world needs more students willing to listen closely to what is being advised – and act on it. The more good coaches we have, the more people who are enabled to understand and deal better with challenging circumstances. Constructive coaching can break open your limitations and free you, like the proverbial butterfly from the chrysalis. The ripple effect is that those who were coached have more energy available to support others and contribute in a positive way to our world. Another benefit is that if you decide to undertake a coaching program yourself, you will make deep and dear friends.

Many people who are not formally life coaches also offer great ideas and support – people like our parents, certain teachers, sports coaches and others. Successful people are also often more generous than you expect. Seek them out and ask for their help; they are rarely threatened by your intention to succeed.

So many people have played a significant and helpful role in my life. You've heard me refer to my father several times; he was my chief mentor during my early years. I would now like to acknowledge three other people who made a big difference to my life.

Grandma Gillman

David and Grandma Gillman, 1988

As a 10 year old I would make a four-kilometre round trip on my bike to Grandma's home. I think I initially went there to be fed (and maybe earn some brownie points). Grandma would cook me lunch of hand-cut chips fried in a pan, eggs and bacon. She always had orange cake on hand, which we would eat with lots of cups of tea. We'd play board games and listen to the football on the crackly quadraphonic radio speakers. And she would listen to my stories about school. She never counselled me, just listened, and it was good to have a refuge when I was stuck at home weekend after weekend and needed to get out of the house – particularly on weekends when Dad couldn't go to the gun club with me.

I think my compassion for people living on their own developed when visiting Grandma. She never quite revealed if she was lonely but I figured that my presence there was good company for her. She passed away in 1998 and I can remember having one vivid dream about her soon after her passing. I was sitting with her at her table in her lounge room and we were having a conversation about how the family was going and how we were affected by her passing. That might sound strange but it's exactly what happened. Even though I missed her physical presence, I knew from that dream that the important people in my life are never really gone.

John Weedon, Headmaster

Year 10, Mr Weedon and David with the Hangar Rat

I used to fear my first headmaster at the Junior School campus. His forehead had been permanently 'scarred' by many years of frowning. But my new headmaster at secondary school, Mr John Weedon, was completely different. Mr Weedon was the master of rapport and would encourage all the students to engage with him. His pleasant and heart-warming magnetism made that easy.

During my first week, he greeted me with a smile, handed me my books, and said, "David Gillman, nice to meet you. You're welcome to come visit me anytime."

I'm not sure if he had a suspicion of what I had experienced in Junior School; I do remember something he said at an opening speech at assembly: "I don't care what happened to you last year at primary school; all I and the staff care about is what you are doing here and now." This allowed me to leave behind some of the baggage I was carrying about past teachers.

Mr Weedon played an important part in building up my confidence. It was he who created the space for me to explore how I could stand out from the other students and contribute to the school rather than adopting my usual strategy of melting into the background. He was supportive of the school's Aero Club; we assembled the school's first radio-controlled aeroplane in Year 9 and flew it on the oval where the jocks were kicking the football. Mr

Weedon even filmed me flying the school's plane over the oval. (It just so happened that in my rush to assemble the plane for flight, I'd put the wings on backwards. It still flew but my god was I embarrassed when I discovered the back-to-front wings when it landed!) He also took the Aero Club out flying at Brimbank Park during lunchtime one day so that all the members could fly the plane while I instructed them. (This teaching experience is possibly what foreshadowed my current interest in coaching).

It is because of Mr Weedon that my character grew. He made all the students feel included and gave every student the attention they deserved. I also feel he helped me develop the belief that pushing on in life meant pursuing a line of nonconformity.

Our last ever conversation was at the school valedictory dinner. I went up to him, shook his hand and told him that he had pretty much saved my life. He looked me in the eye and said, "Thank you, but David, seeing a picture of you up on the projector screen tonight, surrounded by your school friends and making it to the end of Year 12, you have yourself to be thankful for."

He was one of my greatest heroes! When he passed away some time around 1995, there was only standing room at his funeral service at St. John's Uniting Church. Students right throughout his term as headmaster were in attendance.

Eva John: Year 8 Coordinator

Despite her angelic face and kindly look, Mrs John's voice and mannerisms came across as authoritative. There didn't seem to be any time for bullshit from us students. I can't remember her words exactly, but I most certainly remember her demeanour! I had no intention of crossing her although I did challenge her on occasion. When she had to summon me for a conversation about my grades, she was compassionate and softly spoken. I had been expecting some harsh accusations in a very loud tone that would be heard all the way through the adjoining offices but she kept her voice quiet.

The outcome of that meeting was that I was to report to Mrs John's office every two weeks with up-to-date plans for how I was going to complete my homework during those weeks. I didn't share with her about my struggles or thoughts of suicide, I just religiously reported to her, and probably this pattern did help me to establish better study habits.

One day in one of those meetings she gave me my instructions, including a command to lift my game, and I just sat there, despondent. I was starting to formulate a plan of emptying my books out of my locker, going home, and not coming back. This was a time when I had begun to consider suicide again.

I wasn't looking directly at Mrs John but I could see her puzzled expression out of the corner of my eye. There were 5-10 seconds of dead silence, and then she made a fist with her hand and began to knock me on the shoulder. With each second or third 'bump' she said softly but sportingly, "Come on Gill-man… Come on Gill-man… You can do this."

I nodded, thanked her, took my folder, and moped back to class. It didn't hit me until that night that, for the first time, a teacher from my school actually seemed concerned enough to try and bolster my confidence. It's one of the kindest acts I'd ever experienced from the school. Because of that one supportive action (an anchor if you will), I stayed at school. I didn't run.

My last conversation with Mrs John was a decade later at the Melbourne Showgrounds. I came across her in the crowds and for a moment she seemed to be looking at me as if wondering whether she knew me or not. I went straight up to her and introduced myself, and she did remember me. That day I told her, "I'm glad I've had a chance to see you again. I wanted to tell you that I am grateful that you looked out for me in Year 8. You may have saved my life."

She smiled.

Quite a few people 'saved my life' during those difficult years of my childhood and early adulthood. That's because I was on the brink of serious depression or suicide several times. I remain deeply grateful to each one of them.

Express gratitude in your notebook

List your teachers, friends, coaches or mentors and describe how they have each helped you in the past. Did one of them give you a critical piece of advice that saved you from disaster? Was there one action that changed the course of your life? They deserve to know when they are doing well, too, so you might like to express your gratitude directly to them.

If you were to emulate what they did for you, could you pass on what you have learned, and if so, who would you like to help or inspire?

NEW EMPOWERING RULE #30: Appreciate my support systems.

"Keep away from people who try to belittle your ambitions. Small people always do that, but the really great make you feel that you, too, can become great."

– MARK TWAIN

Conclusion

"The best way to predict the future is to create it."

– ABRAHAM LINCOLN

As we approach the end of this book and my journey into the past, I hope that you have gained value from my memories, challenges and insights. I am deeply grateful for everything I've learnt and how I've grown. With the passage of time and all the personal development work I've done, I can see the flip side of experiences I once considered to be a curse.

In the Introduction I stated that 'my near-suicide at age 12 became the lynchpin to my success. My life changed when I realised that the universe or higher power made everything happen *for* me, not just to teach me a lesson or to trip me up.' I acknowledged that that was – is – a very confronting idea. But I am convinced of it. I can see that each of my difficult childhood and young-adult experiences presented me with an opportunity to grow and mature, to develop resilience and resourcefulness and skills.

The first 43 years of my life felt like a roller coaster ride. A generally happy childhood produced naïve ideas about what my teenage years were going to be like; when I reached them and found that they were not going to be what I imagined, I was shocked and became jaded, disillusioned and depressed.

At the age of 12, I had no way of knowing what lay ahead. I was in such deep, dark anxiety, loneliness and depression that it was virtually impossible to see past the next five minutes. Even the next five minutes represented more pain. I had a home, I was being fed, I had parents who hadn't divorced, the factory was still running, there was no war raging in my neighbourhood, I wasn't on drugs, I wasn't being raped ... and yet, my problems were as huge to me as if I *were* being attacked. Being an adolescent, I did not have sufficient experience of dealing with life challenges to manage the ones facing me then.

As you know, I survived that day in August. I was scared. But even as my head was 'going underwater' for the last time, I was holding out hope that my situation would change, that a power outside of me would step in and intervene. Perhaps that hope was all that was needed for me to be able to hear the little inner voice of wisdom that stopped my fearful, mad action and turned me in a healthier direction. Hope, an urgent need to rise above my circumstances, and a leap of faith.

Once I had taken that leap, friends and teachers were waiting to meet me in the future. So yes, I transformed my life, but I didn't rise out of this situation alone. Many wonderful people reached out to me when they saw me struggling. And, ironically, one of the greatest influences on me was Biff himself.

Yes, I took a beating from him. Yes, he often humiliated me. Yes, he probably would have hurt me badly if I'd decided to duke it out with him during other incidents that followed. I was so constantly frustrated that I suspect I was in danger of drifting into the sociopathic end of the spectrum. But Biff's bullying behaviours pushed me to the point where I had to dig deep inside myself to find out what I was made of. I stopped myself from snapping and went on to enjoy a great life.

I am certain that, had I taken Biff's life and gone to prison, I would have developed and locked in those sociopathic tendencies. Between my guilt and the stress of the whole court and prison process, wardens and the other inmates messing with me, and a restricted life when I was finally released, I suspect that I would have hardened into a much tougher character. If I had encountered the thug outside my parents' factory after spending time in prison, would I have been carrying a knife while locking up at night? Would I have used it when I had that thug distracted with my phone? Would I have made things much worse for myself?

Having trudged through difficult times I have always felt willing and eager to help others. But I couldn't have contributed to my friends, family, dance partners, blood donor recipients and other associates if I'd lost my life at the age of 12. *My need to help others is powered by my own pain.*

One of the reasons I was holding that gun in my hand was that I had lost all hope in humanity and in myself. My 12-year-old self had a rose-coloured view of everything from my childhood, so any losses from that period were extremely painful. Whether the loss of kindergarten friends, our dogs being put to sleep in old age, Jo seeming to just disappear from over the road… I struggled with all of those developments. Seeing her fall into the arms of one of my worst bullies was the final nail in my coffin!

J.K. Rowling, creator of the Harry Potter series, was captured on video addressing Harvard graduation students in 2008. During her speech, she reflected on her lowest times when she was so poor that she was on the verge of homelessness. She said: '…*and so rock bottom became a solid foundation on which I rebuilt my life.*'

Rock bottom is an opportunity to 'hit the reset button' and ReWrite the Rules of Your Life. Life may seem to be trying to shut you out of any meaningful existence, but that doesn't mean you have to accept that or give up. Keep practising, as you would a computer game, and seek out others who may have had similar experiences. Look for new alliances and new environments that may be more conducive to your happiness, and act when opportunity presents itself!

It is during your darkest times that your personal rule book will need to change. The way you currently see your life will need to change. Your beliefs and values may need to change. Your strategies for where you need to be and what you need to do may need to change.

In a way I did die at age 12. The David who felt he did not belong in the world did die that day. I moved forward and began, step by step, to create a whole new life beyond that first grave. I didn't write this book for the purpose of patting myself on the back but to give hope to others who may be facing a premature ending in similar circumstances. I wanted to shine a light on what lies beyond that sort of extreme pain. I wanted to urge others to hang in there, to plan and work for the day when your life fulfils and delights you. There are dozens of reasons for contemplating suicide and they might all be valid, but in the end, the decision to live, and live a rich life, is in your hands.

If someone else had walked into the room and found me with that gun in my hands that day they would have taken it away and made me live. But they couldn't have made me embrace life. That was my choice, my decision, albeit one that I had to keep re-making as I stumbled forward.

The same could be said for vengeance and revenge. It may seem as if it will be a great relief to scratch the 'itch' that has been bothering you for ages and lash out at someone, but there is likely to be a very high price to pay for that sense of entitlement. The bullies who have no concept of their actions in the schoolyard, classroom or workplace should keep that in mind. I wrote Chapters 6 and 7 as a warning to bullies.

I am grateful for what I have experienced now. The process I have been through in rebuilding my life and all my experiences, both good and bad, have given me a far greater depth and understanding of human nature than I would have without those experiences. The decision to live has given me the opportunity to become a different man, and I believe a better one.

I hope that my story has been of benefit to you should you be looking to ReWrite the Rules of *your* life from circumstances that may currently seem unfavourable to a life rich in friends, opportunity and achievement.

My oldest friends were waiting to meet me in the future.

My New Empowering Rules

NEW RULE #1: Instead of meekly going along with everything look for ways to express myself, stand out, and be a nonconformist!

NEW RULE #2: Find my past friends, those who share a happier history with me, and choose new friends who share similar values.

NEW RULE #3: Train in self-defence in a secure environment. Seek to build rapport wherever possible with my fellow students. Don't waste any energy trying to appease those who simply wish to use me for their amusement. They're not worth worrying about!

NEW RULE #4: Reach out to an older generation – people I can trust, people I can confide in, maybe someone who has strategies I can use to keep me safe and sane.

NEW RULE #5: Find out what really excites me in life!

NEW RULE #6: Instead of listening to people who don't understand me and frustrate me, I will learn from the history books.

NEW RULE#7: Consciously choose which voice I listen to. Listen To the Most Empowering Voice.

NEW RULE #8: Avoid fighting wherever possible. If it seems there will be no escaping a fight, consider enrolling in self-defence classes.

NEW RULE #9: Think twice before acting in vengeance. When contemplating revenge on anyone, interrupt that pattern by sitting quietly and allowing my mind to coach me to a solution. Weigh up the pros and cons of reacting in anger, and the pros and cons of finding a better response.

NEW RULE #10: Activate the power of my dreams. Take action on them. I deserve it.

NEW RULE #11: Let go of illusions. Leave the past in the past. Take realistic actions to realise my important dreams.

NEW RULE #12: Be humble about receiving honest feedback from those who love me.

NEW RULE #13: Flip the coin! Make fitness and proper diet a priority to give me the leverage to build up my self-esteem and confidence. (The benefits to me far outweigh the pain of self-discipline.)

NEW RULE #14: Honour and respect my body by eating well and exercising regularly. (The benefits to me far outweigh the pain of self-discipline.)

NEW RULE #15: Do the self-development work (eg. Anthony Robbins' questions) because the insights I gain will motivate me to create long-lasting change.

NEW RULE #16: Face old fears and do the things I need to do to achieve closure on old, troubling experiences.

NEW RULE #17: No matter how long it takes or what it takes, hang on to my important dreams and live them. (If I hang on, I will realise those dreams one way or another!)

NEW RULE #18: Instead of allowing myself to be imprisoned by past experiences, keep my mind open to new possibilities.

NEW RULE #19: Take a risk. Get out there and invest in myself.

NEW RULE #20: Keep Trying. Believe in myself. Trust that I am worthy. Have a go. Take wise risks!

NEW RULE #21: Seek knowledge and experience in new fields. These 'new worlds' will open up my mind and skills beyond what I might have imagined possible.

NEW RULE #22: Express gratitude to those who play a pivotal role in my life.

NEW RULE #23: Implement tried and true strategies for success.

NEW RULE #24: Keep my cool and get creative.

NEW RULE #25: Don't bury myself in tragic events outside my range of influence. It is good to be aware of such events but it burns my energy to dwell on these matters when there is nothing I can do about them.

NEW RULE #26: Surround myself with like-minded people. If my current friends or even family don't suit me or can't help me, find new allies with similar needs to mine. (Do my best not to alienate friends and family in the process.)

NEW RULE #27: Invest in a life coach. Life coaches are as important to my growth as a property investment is to my financial future. Invest in myself by looking for the best coach I can find. I may find that the outcome is aspirations and achievements far higher than I can right now possibly imagine!

NEW RULE #28: Appreciate past hurtful experiences.

NEW RULE #29: If forced to forgive, deeply consider how it serves me to forgive. Remember that my resentment poisons *me*, not the other person.

NEW RULE #30: Appreciate my support systems.

I'd love to coach you!

As children being read a bedtime story we were often so caught up in the tale that we imagined ourselves to be one of the characters. The same happens in our own lives: we tell ourselves stories every day, reminding ourselves subconsciously of who we are, who and what matters to us, what we believe about ourselves and others, and more. But we often get so caught up in the current version that we forget to choose a new destination and write a new story to get us there – and that can be a big pity if our story is not an empowering one.

I have been urged, repeatedly, to pass on what I've learned. I'm grateful for my decision to train as a life coach and thus find a really practical way of encouraging others to deal with dark times and make the most of their strengths.

While I am trained and able to coach a range of issues, such as phobias, poor habits and limiting beliefs, my speciality is helping clients to ReWrite The Rules governing their lives, since that is my passion. Bottom line, what is most important and dear to me is to inspire and motivate.

Do you know what it is you are looking for?
Do you feel blocked?
Is a limiting belief holding you back?
Do you think or feel that life is unfair?

You now know that people in their darkest, loneliest hours can turn their lives around as the result of just one idea.

You know what one particular idea meant to a depressed suicidal teenager who was being ridiculed by teachers and fellow students, feeling isolated, and lacking answers to his burning questions.

You know what that idea was worth not just to the future of the teenager but to his family. (After all, he narrowly escaped a prison term).

You know what it meant to him when he was struggling with a weight problem while trying unsuccessfully to find the life partner of his dreams;

while he was continually undermined by a lack of self-belief, was living a small life and not fulfilling his potential…

If I can do it, you can do it.

There are many people who rise from the ashes, people who overcome their challenges and realise their dreams. Reading their stories has always inspired me and given me hope, but the advice of famous stars and world leaders and billionaires is not nearly as inspiring to me as the stories of ordinary people fulfilling their potential. My intention in this book is to inspire you with my 'ordinary-person story', and give you hope as you pursue your goals.

Sometimes we perceive our circumstances as too frightening or overwhelming to even contemplate leaving the comfort of our current reality, but with small regular steps we can make a new reality for ourselves. Small steps are okay! The important thing is to keep moving, growing and exploring your world. One day you will no longer be here, and none of this will matter anymore. But while you're here, honour your life by giving it everything you've got.

What will you accomplish?
What will you discover?
What will you realise?
What will you learn?
What will you experience?

I look forward to hearing from you.

David Gillman
david@keystonecoaching.net
https://www.keystonecoaching.net/
https://www.facebook.com/DavidRGillman/

Ten Painful Truths:

1. The average human life is relatively short.
2. You only ever live the life you create for yourself.
3. Being busy does not mean being productive.
4. Some kind of failure always occurs before success.
5. Thinking and doing are two very different things.
6. You don't have to wait for an apology to forgive.
7. Some people are simply the wrong match for you.
8. It's not other people's job to love you; it's yours.
9. What you own is not who you are.
10. Everything changes, every second.

– COMPILED BY SUE FITZMAURICE

In Gracious Acknowledgement…

On this page I would like to celebrate and recommend some of my coaches.

Kerrie Ward continues to teach at different studios in Melbourne. If you wish to have dance lessons with Kerrie, please contact me through my website.

Duane Brown began Real Life Motivation in Queensland in 2017. Although Duane's particular focus is on helping his clients quit drinking alcohol and smoking, he is a very skilful coach and can assist with other problems and issues as well. Duane's website is: http://reallifemotivation.com or call Duane on 0412 655 028 or (61) 07 32 811634.

R!k Schnabel is the founder of Life Beyond Limits. He has instructed many coaches, teachers and mentors in the theory, practice and power of NLP a methodology that helps people of all ages and backgrounds to create fulfilling empowered lives. It is because of his influence as a teacher and mentor that I wrote this book. One of his very generous acts was staying back one night when class was finished to give me some guidelines for writing a coaching book. R!k has publicly announced that he is retiring from instructing in NLP. He is passing the baton to the many hundreds he has taught.

How do you get what you want and need?

What exciting new possibilities and opportunities might be out there for you?

Whether you're a struggling teenager or an adult with a strong need for change, this is for you.

FOUNDATION FOR SUCCESS

is a short workshop designed to help you achieve your life goals.

Your facilitator, David Gillman, will utilise extremely powerful life coaching tools to assist you in digging deep and breaking through to new levels of success.

Author of *ReWrite The Rules – Turn Your Life Around from Victim to Victorious*, David has transformed his life from misery to mastery.

He will guide you in applying the tools he used to climb out of the pit and create a rich and fulfilling life.

You already have the power. Make it work for you.

Take the first step!
Enrol now for this fun, interactive workshop at
www.keystonecoaching.net
or email David Gillman:
david@keystonecoaching.net

Is the emotional clutter in your life impeding your goals?

Imagine the life you'd have if you were able to focus your time and energy!

It's no secret that following the same old patterns gets us the same old results, so what can we do to break out of the rut?

BREW YOUR OWN SUCCESS

is a comprehensive, in-depth workshop conducted in a supportive classroom environment and led by high-achiever David Gillman.

Brew Your Own Success builds on skills learnt at Foundation For Success, David's introductory workshop. You will explore and shape the key areas of your life.

Take control of your life direction.

Enrol now at www.keystonecoaching.net
or email David Gillman:
david@keystonecoaching.net

www.ingramcontent.com/pod-product-compliance
Lightning Source LLC
Chambersburg PA
CBHW071920290426
44110CB00013B/1428